EATING LIGHTBULBS

MACHETE
Joy Castro, Series Editor

Eating
Lightbulbs

and Other Essays

Steve Fellner

MAD CREEK BOOKS, AN IMPRINT OF
THE OHIO STATE UNIVERSITY PRESS
COLUMBUS

Published by Mad Creek Books, an imprint of The Ohio State University Press.

Library of Congress Cataloging-in-Publication Data

Names: Fellner, Steve, author.

Title: Eating lightbulbs and other essays / Steve Fellner.

Other titles: Machete.

Description: Columbus : Mad Creek Books, and imprint of The Ohio State University Press [2021] | Series: Machete | Summary: "Personal essays detailing the triumphs, traumas, and failures of the author's formative years as a young gay man in the late twentieth century"—Provided by publisher.

Identifiers: LCCN 2021015584 | ISBN 9780814258071 (paperback) | ISBN 0814258077 (paperback) | ISBN 9780814281598 (ebook) | ISBN 0814281591 (ebook)

Subjects: LCSH: Fellner, Steve. | Gay men. | Mothers and sons. | LCGFT: Essays.

Classification: LCC PS3606.E3885 E28 2021 | DDC 814/.6 [B]—dc23

LC record available at https://lccn.loc.gov/2021015584

Cover design by Charles Brock

Text design by Juliet Williams

Type set in Adobe Caslon Pro

for my mother

CONTENTS

I

II

III

IV

V

I

Self-Portrait as a 1970s Cineplex Movie Theatre (An Abecedarian)

Agatha (1979)

It all starts with a single mystery.

And then another. And another. And then another.

I can still remember seeing my mother crying as *Agatha*'s ending credits rolled. My mother said, "My tragic flaw: I hold no mystery."

Agatha is a biopic that offers a theory as to what happened to the mystery writer Agatha Christie during her eleven-day disappearance in 1926. Some said it was a kidnapping. Others a mere publicity stunt. Most recently, it's been said it was a result of amnesia, a psychogenic trance. *Agatha* claims that she left to plot the murder of her philanderer husband. "Not everything revolves around a man," my mother said.

Good parenting, my mother believed, was solving any stupid mystery. Sex only causes trouble. Death is a bore. A story always needs many ends.

Ben (1972)

I was obsessed with the title song to *Ben*. It has a young Michael Jackson crooning lyrics like "We both found what we were looking for. With a friend to call my own, I'll never be alone . . ." And, "I used to say I and me, now it's us, now it's we." I knew the lyrics by heart.

There was a man I loved. I didn't know how to tell him I loved him. His name was Ben, too. It was the '90s. *Ben* was released in the '70s. There was no way he would link the two.

I wrote out all the lyrics and told him that I had written a poem for him. As I read it, he gave me a funny look. "Are you sure you wrote that song?" he said.

"Of course. It took me weeks."

There was a long pause. "That's the song from that movie about killer rats. It's about some loser who has nothing. So he befriends a rat. A rat. Is his only friend." He enunciated that last part very, very slowly.

"Really?" I said.

"Really," he said. "You know what? I don't get with liars." He walked out of my apartment.

The next day, there was a cage covered with a sheet on my front porch. I could hear some frantic scraping. It was a rat. And not the pet-store, domesticated kind; it was a back-alley rat, black-furred and crazy with fear. There was a note that said: "LOVE THIS, YOU ASSHOLE!"

Coma (1978)

When I had my first manic episode, I couldn't sleep. I tried and tried. I took sleeping pills, listened to music, exercised for hours, drank warm milk, devoured melatonin, whatever it took. I stayed up all night long for three days and watched TV. Once *Coma* was on. It's a mystery/thriller revolving around a series of healthy people who mysteriously go brain-dead after minor surgeries.

This was all I could think: *They are so lucky. They are so lucky.*

Deliverance (1972)

In *Deliverance*, Burt Reynolds plays a beefy alpha male who is obsessed with seeing the Cahulawassee River before it's turned into one huge lake. He takes his posse river rafting; they meet various and dangerous people along their way. My favorite one: a deformed, silent banjo kid. Everybody remembers the "squeal like a pig" guy in *Deliverance*, but the banjo kid, he doesn't need a catchphrase. He never speaks. He just strums. One of the guys in Reynolds's crew has his own banjo. They go back and forth and back again, calling and responding to each other for a scene that lasts for over five minutes. You would never expect music to be in a place so remote, so distant.

Once I had a dream and all I could hear were those banjos being strummed, the strain of the strings, and then the death of silence. It's the one time in my life I wondered if God had spoken to me.

Every Which Way but Loose (1978)

I always wanted to own a pet. The closest thing I've ever gotten was a goldfish. My brother named it Doorbell. Every morning he would get up and feed it. He'd say, "Hi, Doorbell. How are you doing today?" The fish never answered, but that never stopped him from asking the question.

One day we went and saw *Every Which Way but Loose*, a star vehicle for Clint Eastwood who plays a tough guy roaming around the American West looking for a lost lover. Of course, the real star of the movie is his best friend, an orangutan named Clyde. Clyde and Eastwood have a perfect comic rapport.

When we got home from the movie, my brother changed the name of his goldfish from Doorbell to Clyde. A few weeks later the fish died. I told my brother it was from natural causes. I lied. I still think the cause of death was identity confusion.

Fiddler on the Roof (1971)

When I saw the movie in high school, I convinced my drama director to do the play. I wanted to be the lead. I wanted to play the role that Zero Mostel made famous. Operatic in nature, always larger than life, I wanted to be Tevye. I wanted to be the ultimate Jewish patriarchal figure who ruled over his family with an ironclad fist, refusing to assimilate.

I didn't let the fact that I was supposed to be Catholic stop me. If I had to convert to Judaism to get the lead role in the school play, so be it.

The first day of the production I lost my voice. "God isn't on your side," my director said. I prayed to God to help me. There was no answer. No voice, no fiddle playing coming from the roof or anywhere else. And, this time, not even a banjo.

The Godfather (1972)

This is a fact: The horse's head was real. The horse had died and they cut it off and froze it and then brought it to the set. Jesus Christ.

The things people will do for art.

I can never remember anything in the scene other than the horse's head. Not even the basics, really: I know an Italian mafioso wakes up to find blood in the sheets and then the wrapped towels at the end of the bed. And then something else happens, and so on and so forth. There are a lot of famous scenes in *The Godfather*. But all I remember is that head of the horse.

Am I allowed to say it? Once I dreamt that I was the head of the horse. My eyes did not blink. My mouth did not move. All I could feel was the angry freezer burn of the ice.

H. O. T. S. (1979)

I remember asking my father to tell me about the birds and the bees. I don't think I really even cared to hear about sex. I was just curious about the metaphors. Who were the bees and who were the birds? It might have been an obvious correlation, but still. I loved my father. I wanted to hear it from him.

My father looked a little puzzled when I asked the question. He grabbed a newspaper, scanned the movie listings and said, "This one looks good. It'll tell you more about the birds and the bees than I can."

H. O. T. S. is a stupid softcore sex comedy that features Danny Bonaduce from *The Partridge Family*. It also stars three Playboy Playmates. My father told me their names. I couldn't remember them. In the movie, they were in some kind of sorority and they wore tight shirts and red shorts. (My father later bragged to me regarding his theory about their uniforms. "I think the owners of Hooters must have ripped them off. They're practically identical.")

I kept on almost falling asleep during the movie. My father was spellbound. He nudged me a few times because I was snoring too loud.

It was the first time I told my father I was gay.

At that time, I was happy I never had to use the words.

I Spit on Your Grave (1978)

When I was an undergraduate, I rented a videotape of *I Spit on Your Grave*. The film focuses on a young woman who is raped and beaten by a group of men who she later runs down and kills one by one. I'm not sure why I thought it would make a good date movie.

My boyfriend fell asleep during the film. I had to nudge him every so often to keep him from snoring. I was pissed.

I'm a hypocrite. If I fall asleep in a movie, that's fine. But when someone else does, it infuriates me.

"How could you nod off during that film?" I asked.

"I'd rather not see this kind of shit," he said. "Something happened to me a long time ago. I never fought back."

Once he said that, I knew we would never go on another date again. I needed to believe I was the only one who suffered in certain ways. I needed to have a secret. And I didn't want to share mine. We broke up after that night. I never saw him again.

The Jerk (1979)

My husband's father died weeks before we started dating. His father's favorite movie was *The Jerk*. I had never seen it.

The movie stars Steve Martin as a loser who is an adopted son of a black family of Mississippian sharecroppers. When he comes to the realization that he is tone-deaf, he is forced to face the fact that he doesn't belong and sets out on his own adventures to find love and success.

I watch my husband watch the movie. He tells me what his father's favorite jokes were. I don't know if he realizes that a lot of the ones are what he would have found funny anyway, without his father's cues. So I watch my husband watching this movie through his father's eyes. Does he experience this silly slapstick comedy as a profane, necessary elegy? I do.

Kramer vs. Kramer (1979)

"They make the movie so dramatic. Like divorce is a big tragedy. Like it warrants a two-hour-plus running time," my mother said. "You can boil it down to two scenes: when he stops saying 'I love you' and when she says 'Leave.' No one deserves an Academy Award for that script. I could have written it. After all, I lived it."

Love Story (1970)

Even I cry during this dishonorable tearjerker. But the one thing that really bothers me is that after Ali MacGraw's character dies, and Ryan O'Neal leaves the hospital, the drama then turns into a resolution of a father-son conflict. Instead, I wanted the movie to focus on the period of time it takes O'Neal to walk from the hospital bed to his car. I wanted them to film it in real time, so we see O'Neal walking and walking and walking, for maybe twenty minutes. No dialogue. When I imagine grieving over my husband Phil's death, that's what I see as the most difficult distance: the bed he dies in and the exit to the hospital. I imagine thinking that as long as I don't leave the building, he is not dead. I imagine hiding in nurses' stations, bathrooms, storage rooms for days on end, thinking if I'm not found, he is not lost.

Magic (1978)

Who wouldn't be excited by seeing Anthony Hopkins play a ventriloquist tortured by a murderous dummy?

How I've always craved to be someone's puppet. I've longed for dummies with sculpted bodies. All jerks and pulling and strings. The pleasure of being moved by the hands of a familiar stranger. The pleasure of not having to think of words. The pleasure of making noise for someone else's satisfaction.

Norma Rae (1979)

Once I went to human resources to complain about the way I was being treated. I was told to talk to someone named Lisa who was in charge. I wanted to be able to have a genuinely fair shot at overtime work just like everybody else. Lisa asked me to tell her my story. "Every single detail," she said. I told her every single detail.

"You feel better?" she asked.

"Why would I feel better?" I said. "I still don't have what I deserve."

"Sometimes it feels good just to tell your side of the story," she said. I walked out of the office and decided that I needed to contact a union rep. I imagined myself as a contemporary Norma Rae. I imagined myself standing on a large conference table with a huge, unwieldy sign that said "Union." I imagined being so proud about the way the magic marker made the most beautiful lines.

The union rep listened to my side of the story. "Tell me every single detail," he said.

I told him every single detail.

"You have a case," he said.

I was happy. He said that we'd meet with Lisa and find out how I could be given an equal opportunity. "I'll be there for you, for support," he said.

Before the meeting, I decided I wanted to look like Norma Rae. I put gel in my hair and pulled it back. I practiced angry and determined looks in the mirror.

When the three of us met to talk, the union rep completely changed his tune from what he'd told me only a day earlier on the phone. He now said I didn't have a case. He said he'd chatted with Lisa. They reviewed every single detail and realized everything was completely fine, nothing to worry about. He smiled. "Sorry," the union rep and Lisa said in near-unison. "But if you want to tell us your story again, please do. It's always good to have an emotional release."

If I were Sally Field, I guess at that moment I would have climbed up onto Lisa's desk. But the "Union" sign I held up would now have a big question mark at the end.

One Flew over the Cuckoo's Nest (1975)

I wanted to be Nurse Ratched. I was obsessed with her nurse's uniform: the aggressive whiteness, the tough material, the stubborn zipper, the perfect creases. Everything was surface and hidden threat. I could never imagine her taking off her cap. She rolled out of bed with it on. Her skin was dull sheen. Like the floors she walked on. Like the windows the patients stared out of.

She was a woman who always had a destination. She never looked around. She always looked forward. She was a woman who had mastered the art of locking a door: She knew never to look back.

I admired the way she watched the patients swallow their pills. Follow the rules. Under her watch, no one would choke.

You could hear the broken silence of something going down their throat.

She was all about time, the clicking of a clock.

She was the measurement, the fit, the pattern. Numbers came as easy to her as madness did for her patients.

Corrections were not things she believed in. They were the work of the devil, an unbalanced mind, a patient with the wrong number of pills. She was as large as God. The sound of her shoes on the bare floor: the echo of wounded angels landing.

The Paper Chase (1973)

I worshipped John Houseman's performance as the brilliant, didactic, intimidating law professor Dr. Charles W. Kingsfield Jr. in *The Paper Chase.* I've always wanted to scare students into intellectual submission. How can you not have admiration for Dr. Kingsfield? During the first class period of the semester, he immediately puts one of his students on the spot, relentlessly using the Socratic method, humiliating him in front of a jam-packed lecture hall.

Now I am an English professor and I try to think of things Dr. Kingsfield would say. This is one of the best lines I've created. When I compliment students on their writing, they'll often say thank you. My response: "That was not a compliment. It was a fact. Never thank me again."

If a student doesn't show up to class and asks me if they missed anything important, I say, "Every single thing I say is important. Class is sixty minutes long. You missed at least sixty crucial things to your development as a writer and, by extension, a human being."

There's a part of them that believes me. So: I believe them. And that's why I choose to be a teacher.

Quadrophenia (1979)

I was never the rebel. I was scared of people who could change their lives on a dime, like Jimmy Cooper in *Quadrophenia*. He jettisons his "respectable" career as a post-room boy in a firm to be a London Mod, a gang leader.

I do, however, like the idea of having definite rivals. Mod or Rocker? Rocker or Mod? Make your decision, boy. Which are you? It's hard to make mistakes in life when your enemies are clearly marked.

Of course, it never turns out the way you want it. In *Quadrophenia*, during a violent fight, a member in one of the rival gangs dies, and it turns out that it's Jimmy's best friend. He doesn't stick around. He takes off.

Just as Jimmy thinks he's escaped from his former disrupted and disappointing life, he ends up being catapulted over a ditch on his motorbike. The ending is a little ambiguous. While some say the beginning of the film hints that Jimmy survives, others have argued that Jimmy kills himself in that final scene.

Curiously, the director of the film didn't find out until it was too late: The same location was the site of a real-life suicide.

Rollerball (1975)

Once I asked a colleague: "Do you think I'd be a good dad?" to which he replied: "A perfect pushy stage mom. A dad, no. But Phil could be."

I fantasize about Phil, myself, and a child—our child—holding hands, an invincible trio, roller-skating with sheer bravado past the skyscrapers full of evil Republicans.

That's the movies for you: giving you defenses you'll never have.

People always ask us if we're going to have a child. They always tell Phil he'd be such a good dad. And he would. If some malicious goon came darting toward our kid on a roller rink, Phil would swoop the child away with perfect timing. Also, he has patience.

Sometimes I think to myself: *I am so sorry, Phil.* And then: *I wish I wasn't gay. I could be so much more.* And then: *Shut the hell up, you idiot.*

We have stuffed animals that we put to bed at night. One by one. We have a teddy bear that we call Mr. Pokey. We give him little adventures.

Smokey and the Bandit (1977)

When I think of the movie *Smokey and the Bandit*, I think of wind. I do not think about the silly plot involving a massive car race over a tractor trailer of beer. I do not think of Sally Field and Burt Reynolds and the lack of spark in their romance. I do not think of the brilliant editing, showing us the hot pursuits with precise cross-cutting.

There is nothing more beautiful than wind. Perhaps this is why I am afraid to drive. In *Smokey and the Bandit*, I like watching the wind tousling the hair of the actors, and sending the vehicles into a tailspin, or disappearing feet before the flag falls at the end of the race. I imagine the wind as God's breath, overtaking my car, blowing me to the heavens above. The wind reaches everything. No movie, even *Smokey and the Bandit*, can quite capture the wind's stillness or its aggression, its fierce determination to do what no human can: move beyond itself.

The Texas Chain Saw Massacre (1974)

Everyone thinks there's so much blood in this movie. But whenever I see the film, I'm always in awe how little of it there actually is. In fact, there is none. For me, the scariest moment has nothing to do with any sort of gore. This is the setup: We see one of the women who escaped from Leather-face in the forest. She runs into a gas station/convenience store. She's scared to death. She has forgotten to close and lock the door. She hides behind the counter. She gets up and tries to see if he's coming. It's dead silent. She waits. And waits. As we do. And we already know she will soon be dead, and she pretty likely knows it, too.

Death is not a cheap scare. Death is not a lot of dumb shocks. Death is the moment between waiting for something to happen and what happens when it does.

Up in Smoke (1978)

Cheech and Chong were my heroes. I remember catching their debut *Up in Smoke* on late-night cable. The Latino comedians inspired me to try to light my first bong. My hands were awkward and the fire singed my best friend Sean's hair and burned his ear.

I thought for sure our friendship was over. How can you profess to care for someone after you almost killed them for a dumb puff? The comedy duo possessed a certain grace when they handed the bong back and forth, inhaling and exhaling with a perfect rhythmic intensity. It wasn't something you could learn. It was a God-given gift. They had the perfect rapport. No woman got in their way.

Years ago I found out they had broken up. It ended in a truly nasty, irreconcilable way. How could my friendship still remain if theirs didn't?

Sean and I never looked at each other blurry-eyed and hungry, laughing over nothing, wrapped in a cloud of sweet air. We were sober and desperate, marching through smokeless gay bars. We took nothing into our lungs, nothing even approached our hearts, except for the fumes of bad cologne and stale poppers.

Viva Knievel! (1977)

Imagine being the most talented motorcycle stuntman in the history of the world and finding out that villainous people are luring you to Mexico, where they want to kill you and then pack cocaine in your corpse for easy traveling over country borders. You know, that old story.

How good it would feel to do jumps and flips and wheelies like Evil Knievel, all in the name of escape and transcendence.

Sometimes Mr. Knievel doesn't even hold onto the handlebars. I guess that's my tragic flaw: I always do. And my grasp is always too tight.

A Woman under the Influence (1974)

I can still remember the first time I saw Gena Rowlands as Mabel in *A Woman under the Influence*. She's suffering from severe mental illness. The first half of the movie focuses on her preparing dinner for a dozen men in her husband's construction crew. You can see how untethered she is. Everything sends her reeling. We don't know if she's going to make it past serving them an initial drink.

The next time we see her she has just been discharged from a psychiatric hospital. Her family has thrown her a welcome-home party. It's a nice idea. But the sheer pressure of having to show gratitude and joy overwhelms her. She's probably been pushed over the edge again. We don't know for sure. The movie ends before we are certain.

Like most of Cassavetes's films, the scenes go on and on. There are only two set pieces in the entire movie: the kitchen table and the living room where the party takes place. Once I got a stopwatch and timed how many seconds it took before Mabel started to go truly mad.

I recorded it in my journal.

I liked to keep track of madness. I liked to see when it was, exactly, that she broke. I needed to know the demarcation between sanity and doom. I didn't know it then, but I was preparing to cross that line myself.

If you think about the movies that mean the most to you, every single scene of your favorite becomes meaningful foreshadowing, and, equally, every moment becomes a useless epilogue, not enough to hold on to when the film, suddenly, ends.

X, Y, and Zee (1972)

The setup: A rich man (Michael Caine) who is married to a rich woman (Elizabeth Taylor) falls in love with a young rich woman (Susannah York).

What the directors failed to realize: You can't create a measured, precise three-way love triangle if one of the lovers is Elizabeth Taylor. No offense to Susannah York, but more than one point of the triangle has to matter. Elizabeth

Taylor is the point. The single point. She's always the point of any movie she is in. Nothing else matters, no matter how exquisite the shape, no matter how ruined the lines of the triangle may be.

Young Frankenstein (1974)

I was obsessed with Marty Feldman's eyes. I wanted to hold them in my hands. There was something beautiful in their huge, bulbous nature. I imagined putting them on my desk, like small paperweights. I liked the idea of them looking at me as I looked at the world. It was the closest thing to poetry I could imagine.

Zardoz (1974)

I've never liked collecting movie stills. I like to keep the images in my head, altering whatever I want for my satisfaction.

But I do own one. It's from *Zardoz,* a sci-fi movie that takes place in 2035. Sean Connery plays the hero. I've watched the film three times and still cannot explain the plot in any concise way. There are so many characters that if you asked even the best Mormon genealogist, he'd quit his job and just laugh bitterly to himself every time Pioneer Day rolled around. Let's just say this: *Zardoz* involves well-intentioned assassins, phony gods, magic stones, badly staged fight scenes, and a secret society of immortals.

But I don't really care what happens in the movie. That's not what's important.

What matters is Sean Connery's costume.

He is scantily clad in a flaming red bandolier and matching jock strap, knee-high black boots. His hair is in a ponytail. It is, perhaps, the single strangest costume ever worn by a major male Hollywood star in an action movie.

Some might say this is a bungled attempt by Connery to draw attention to himself as a groovy '70s sci-fi hero. Others might say it was a way for him (or the director) to publicly work out private sexual kinks.

But a rare few might simply call it stripping down and getting ridiculous for no other reason than a profoundly mad love for the movies.

I keep the picture on my writing desk. For inspiration.

Eating Lightbulbs

I wanted to eat lightbulbs. I wanted to hear my teeth crunch the little pieces. I wanted to swallow them. I wanted to feel them cutting the insides of my throat.

On some days, lightbulbs scared me. There is a light directly above my treadmill. When I ran, I was afraid that the lightbulb would burst and some pieces would pierce my skin. Maybe one would even make its way into my eye, blinding me. During my exercise, I would unscrew the lightbulb and put it on the dryer, and then get back on. Everything would be fine for a few minutes until I realized that there was the possibility the lightbulb would roll onto the floor and then crack. My husband Phil would hear the noise, and then yell at me, I imagined, for not keeping the lightbulb in a safe space. "Why are you down here in the dark?" he'd say. "You're going to trip and break your neck."

*

I told my psychiatrist about my run-ins with lightbulbs. She wasn't as amused as I pretended to be. "Why do you think you're having these thoughts about lightbulbs? What's a lightbulb standing in for?" she asked.

That's when I knew I hated her. I needed to find a new psychiatrist. I humored her and offered some possibilities. I felt bad for her. If she failed me, no doubt she had failed a lot of other people. It's not like I was anything special.

I told her that I'm afraid of the dark. When I was a child, I would curl up in bed, my blanket over my head, and no matter how hot it got, I would not come up for air. I'd sweat. I'd anticipate the morning when my mother would turn on the lights.

I told her that my dad worked for Commonwealth Edison. He was a meter reader. Perhaps the lightbulb was a stand-in for my father. I was sad. I was processing our relationship, which had been estranged for a number of years. (Happily, it's now better than it has ever been.)

I told her that when I was young I used to burn myself. I liked the way the skin peeled back.

I told her a lot of things. I can't remember a lot of them. All I remember is the resentment in trying to find a metaphor for her. Perhaps madness is when you can't control what you're substituting things for. Everything becomes something else and you lose track of the literal, the real. Or you believe that the real was never there to begin with, and that begins the descent into paranoia and anxiety.

I don't know. After I started to rehabilitate myself, I began to grow resentful toward metaphor. The Universe, I made myself believe, is a beautiful and troubled thing. And no matter how troubled, metaphors are a lie; the people who feel the need to use them are weak. To use metaphor is to sin against the Universe. God has made everything so unique you can't replace something with something else.

Maybe I believe that. Maybe I don't. All I know is that metaphor lurks in places that I never willingly want to go again.

On Redemption

Two days after Luke, my boyfriend, was gay bashed, he broke up with me. He insisted it had nothing to do with The Incident. That was what we called the gay bashing: The Incident. "You weren't even there," Luke said.

I remember making a list of all the things it could be: my occasional failure to shower; my inescapable habit of leaving dental floss all around the apartment; my annual costume party where people had to dress up as a wounded animal; my elbowing him whenever he called me "darling" in public; my periodontal disease; my obsessions with Zima and Yahtzee, etc.

"I'm not a bad person," I said. "I may have done a bad thing or two."

"Is that a confession?" Luke asked.

"What do I have to apologize for?" I said.

"You can keep Gesundheit," he said. Gesundheit was our bunny. I gave it to him as a birthday present. A pet store was closing and there was a huge sign announcing big sales. When I walked inside, I saw the bunny. It was scared. It needed a home. Our home.

"I always hated that dumb bunny," Luke said.

*

The break-up occurred in May, which I appreciated. I figured I had until August to feel better. That was when school began again. Teaching was exhausting. I had no other way of making money. I had to be functional.

During that time, I discovered what depression was. It played tricks with my memory. When I was in the kitchen, I'd put something down and forget where I put it. I'd run around and try to find it and I eventually would, but it would take time. My memory caused me other problems. I like to gossip. More than once a friend told me a secret, and then I repeated it back to them, swearing secrecy, thinking someone else had said it. It didn't take them long to realize I was betraying them. I lost a few friends. Fortunately, I didn't care. I was depressed. No one else's story mattered.

*

Luke and I met in a women's studies course. Back then most classes didn't have a definite focus on gays and lesbians. You took a women's studies course and hoped that someone would make passing mention of something queer-related. That's why I decided to minor in it. Not to mention sometimes a closeted, repressed homo took one, claiming it was to fulfill a general education requirement. But I knew why other men were there. And they knew the reason: to meet a sensitive man. A gay man.

An advanced feminist theory course brought Luke and I together. I sat behind him. One day I wasn't feeling well. I was coughing. He took a small pack of tissues out from his front pocket. I couldn't stop replaying the image: a grown man storing a small pack of tissues in his front pocket. For emergencies. It was the most beautiful thing I had ever seen. I wanted to marry him. I like people who think ahead.

"Do you want a tissue?" he said. I loved that he said tissue instead of Kleenex. It was so elegant.

How could I refuse?

"Yes," I said.

And I said yes to other things. Like going to a Bonnie Tyler concert on acid. Like auditioning for the role of a magician's assistant. Like trying to sleep with the same history professor. Like eating dog food just for the hell of it. Like tricking my adoptive mother into thinking that my biological one called me up and asked to borrow a kidney. Like working at Kmart for one day and then quitting. Like daring someone to walk home from a secluded, distant gay bar in the dead of night.

*

August came pretty quickly. My classes were unremarkable. Except for a college freshman named Jeremy who sat front and center in my composition course. He was an A student. All he did whenever I spoke—beginning with the very first word I uttered to the last—was take notes. It was unnerving.

Because I was still suffering from the break-up, nothing seemed to matter, especially teaching students what a thesis is. I remember saying that a thesis is a promise. You declare what you are going to say in the rest of the paper. And then you need to follow through.

Nothing earth-shattering. But he scribbled it down on his notepad. He wrote with a pencil. I was always waiting for the tip to crack. He wrote with such feverish intensity, it seemed inevitable.

I started to become paranoid. Was Jeremy the child of an important administrator? Had they put a mole in my class as an attempt to find and fire the less effective teachers?

My depression was still causing memory problems. I knew I was offering the class platitudes: "Writing is rewriting!" and "Think of writing as process, not product!" But at least they were heartfelt.

Jeremy's note-taking was a good thing. I began to feel my life had purpose; I looked forward to going to class. I had something to prove and protect: my job. I even bought myself a gradebook; I wanted to track my class's intellectual progress alongside my emotional one. In the past, I usually just put their grades on a piece of loose-leaf notebook paper. Which I then lost. At the end of the semester, I guesstimated their grades, always inflating them. No one ever complained.

One day I felt impulsive and almost approached Jeremy, telling him that the relentless note-taking helped me more than he could imagine. I wasn't sure if that was an appropriate thing to do; it might make him feel self-conscious. Or make me appear lecherous. I promised myself I wouldn't do anything like that. In fact, I remember thinking that I wouldn't look down at him or his notes again. Of course, I didn't keep my vow. I looked down.

At the top of a new, blank page, I saw a single word: FAGGOT.

*

After the first few weeks of the semester, Luke moved out of our apartment. He wanted a new place. Which upset me. I wanted to leave first. I always want to be the first one to leave any occasion: parties, departmental meetings, exercise class, etc. I like to imagine people just the way I left them.

He found a new boyfriend named Rich. Rich possessed the worst trait every ex fears: kindness.

I hated him. Once they invited me over for dinner. We drank good wine. All three of us had a natural rapport. In fact, Luke felt so comfortable that he left Rich and me alone.

"You really seem like a good couple," I said. "Better than we ever were."

"I don't think you can compare relationships," Rich said. "He loves you still."

"You can compare," I said. "And no, he doesn't love me anymore."

There was a pause. "You're right," Rich said. "You have to move on. You have to move on *now*."

*

I tried to put the word FAGGOT out of my mind whenever I saw Jeremy. He could have written the word for any number of reasons. For all I knew, he might have been taking a women's studies course; there was usually a lesson at some point in the semester about reclaiming words that were normally meant to dehumanize. Like the way homosexuals began to use the pink triangle. Or a feminist campus organization naming themselves SLUTS AGAINST RAPE. Or maybe he was passing notes with a kid in another class, prior to mine—straight or gay—and the word was written as an affectionate sign off. Like when you call your best friend a geek or a loser.

Of course, I became even more obsessed with Jeremy. He wasn't particularly attractive—at least twenty pounds overweight, squinty eyes, psoriasis. But I liked his voice. I was convinced I had heard it somewhere before. But I wasn't sure. My anxiety was going down yet I was sure a few brain cells were being killed here and there.

One day after class, Jeremy came up to me and said, "Have we met before?" I was thankful that he didn't ask me the question in front of another student. It sounded like a pickup line. Or at least I needed to hear it that way.

*

I was a member of a Gay and Lesbian Speakers Bureau. People from all over campus would invite us to speak to various groups and classes. They wanted us to share our experiences as homosexuals.

I like talking about myself. So I enjoyed it. It was also a way of possibly meeting someone who wanted to date you because of your confidence. I had been trying to encourage Luke to come with me. I thought it would be a good idea for people to hear about The Incident. But he refused. He didn't tell anyone. Except the police who found him beaten in the middle of the road.

The leader of a Coming Out Support Group invited me to talk. I went.

I told my signature coming out story. I was a freshman in college. My roommates moved out of my dorm room. They thought I was gay. I denied it. I was alone. One night someone slid a copy of *Harper's Magazine* underneath my door. On the cover was a headline from a feature story about coming out. I was doomed. Everyone on my floor knew I was keeping a secret. Now they were torturing me. I called up my mother. She was cranky. She said she was having a bad day. I said that I was having a worse day. She said she was sure hers was worse. I said that mine was undeniably, inarguably worse. "I'm a faggot," I said. And then I hung up the phone. And then I went to the bathroom and saw that there were dozens and dozens of stacks of *Harper's Magazine*. Everyone in the dorms received a complimentary issue that someone slid underneath all the doors.

Everyone laughed. I was a hit.

But I couldn't control myself. I had to tell them more. I told them about The Incident. Except I said I was the one who was beaten. I pretended that I was Luke who was kicked and hit by three men who called him a cocksucker, a fudge packer, a faggot.

The leader of the Coming Out Support Group came up to me afterward and said, "You were really depressing. Please never come back again."

*

One day in class, I was looking at Jeremy, and I saw something I never expected to see: the soul of a gay basher, one of the young men who beat my ex-boyfriend. True, I thought a lot of things that weren't logical at that time. But there was something different about this connection. He did call me a faggot after all.

I knew Luke was happy in his new relationship; he wouldn't want to revisit the past. But it didn't matter. I had found one of his attackers. He had to know. Of course, I hadn't seen the men up close. But still.

After some pleading, Luke agreed to stand outside my classroom and see if it was him. I could feel his reluctance. But I could also feel love. Love makes you overcome your reluctance. Maybe he still loved me. Rich was wrong. Luke was saving me, I convinced myself, as I was saving him. We were both protecting each other. There was no doubt about it. We had each other's back.

*

This is what happened the night of The Incident. Luke and I had been fighting. We needed to get out of the apartment; tensions were high. We went to a bar called A Hole in the

Wall. It was fairly far from where we lived. But we always ended up there. Luke said it was because the drinks were cheap. I thought it was because of its catchy name.

Once we were at the bar, Luke ditched me. In fact, he tossed me his coat and told me to drop our stuff off at the coat check. Which I did. And then for fifteen minutes, I walked around the bar looking for him. He was talking to someone else. "Thanks for leaving me behind," I said.

"Why are you looking at me like that?" Luke said.

"Because."

"Maybe you and I aren't working out," he said and stormed out of the bar.

I ran after Luke. In the parking lot, I said, "I'm going home alone."

"So am I. I'm walking," he said.

"Yes," I said. "Yes, you are."

He dared me to let him walk home without me. I told him to go. It was a long walk. There was no way he was going to do it. He spat at me and then disappeared into the darkness.

He didn't know I was walking behind him. I could tell he was trying to ditch me. Just in case. He marched through the darkest alleys and unlit sections of town. It was raining hard. I didn't know what to say, so I kept hiding in the shadows. This went on for what felt like a good mile.

Then I heard someone shout "Cocksucker!" Someone else yelled "Fudge packer!" Out of nowhere, a van appeared and skidded several feet from Luke. He didn't move.

No one saw me. I was hiding behind some trees.

Three men got out and pushed him against the hood of the van. They punched him until he fell to the ground. One of them took a bat out of the back seat and hit him in the stomach. Another one demanded that he take off his shirt.

I don't know why he made him take off his shirt. But he did.

Two of the men spat on him. And then one kicked him in the stomach. Luke never made any noise.

I kept thinking: *You stupid faggot. You get what you deserve.*

Would the men have stopped if he had made some noise? Why couldn't he show them that he was a victim? Was he *that* weak? As I watched the men kick his body, that's what went through my mind: *Tell them you are in pain. Let them know they are doing a good job hurting you.*

This is what else I thought: *This is God's way of telling you to stay with me. God made you a victim so you would be open to receiving my love.*

But he didn't make a noise.

I still remember the crack of the bat, the thud of his body, the sound of the slap. All I remember is this: I watched three men beat my boyfriend in the middle of a deserted road. I hid behind some trees.

And then I ran. I left him behind. He never saw me.

I remember everything.

*

It turned out I was right. Jeremy was there that night. After Luke visited my class, he took me out for a drink. "Jeremy was the guy I flirted with," he said. "Before The Incident happened."

"You followed me that night," Luke said. "You saw those men. That's why you've been trying to place him."

"Does it matter?"

"No," Luke said. And then he kissed me on the forehead. And then he hit me.

*

For the rest of the semester, I avoided Jeremy. He tried to talk to me a few times, even asking me to look at his notes. He wanted affirmation that he was getting the main points correct. I told him I was busy. He was a solid A student. It was good for me to ignore him. Toughen him up a bit. Your boss doesn't double-check your work. Sometimes you get things wrong. Sometimes you get things right and your boss gets things wrong.

Life is like that. Some things are arbitrary.

That's why I gave him a C+ on his final exam. He got every question right, wrote a perfect essay. But I wanted to teach him something. Perfect grades can only take you so far. The C+ lowered his grade to an A−. I was doing him a favor.

*

I've always had a fantasy of being in an office with a bad student and telling them I hate them.

I would say it just like that: "I hate you."

The student would look a bit shocked and ask me what I just said.

"I hate you," I'd say, "I really, really hate you."

He'd say, "Why?

I'd say, "Because."

"You can't talk to me like that."

"Of course I can. No one else is here."

"But what did I do?"

"You made me grade your paper. You made me spend time with something you think is proof that you have a soul."

*

Of course, Jeremy called my office when the grade reports were released. He was upset. I didn't return his phone call until he called the department head, who called me. "I must have been calling the wrong number," I said.

Jeremy asked, "I thought I did good on the final."

"You did," I said. "Way above average. You got a C+."

"Way above average?"

"That plus means you're not average. You're something special."

That's when he started crying. "What are you doing?" he said.

"Doing what?"

"I can hear it in your voice. Don't do it. Have mercy."

At first, I didn't relent. But the more he talked, the more each word felt like a blow to my stomach; each plea, a swing at my head; each request, a thud against the ground. At least that's what I think I should have felt. I don't know if I did. All I remember is that his words were leaving a smaller space in my memory for Luke who was beaten by horrible men in the middle of a deserted road.

And then, all I felt was annoyance at having to change a tiny thing I had done, something so insignificant I would forget it the next day, or within the next week or two, something that would erase a few dots on a piece of paper, a stupid grade, a verdict with no bearing on anyone's future.

II

No

"You're a man," the woman said to me in front of the meeting room for the sexual abuse support group. "We never expected one to attend. You're our first."

I always like being a first. "Thank you," I said.

"It wasn't a compliment," the woman said. "Just stating a fact."

"My name is Steve," I said. I reached out to shake her hand. I didn't know if that was the right thing to do. There was a period in my life when I feared the touch of any human being: the dread of skin against skin, a kind pat on the shoulder, a hug, even accidentally kicking someone's leg underneath a table. I didn't want to scare her. I didn't want to ask her to do something that I once couldn't do myself.

She gripped my hand in hers. It was a strong, confident shake. I liked her already.

"Nice to meet you," she said. "My name is Olive. We can always use a new member. Even if it is a man."

"I'm gay," I blurted out. I didn't know what else to say. I wanted her to like me.

"You're still a man," she said.

"I guess so," I said. "I guess I am."

*

Within days, Olive and I became best friends. That's how things work with me. I waste no time in courting someone who could be a part of my surrogate family. Life is too short. Plus if you don't move fast enough, there's the chance of another gay man intruding on your territory.

She told me that she didn't feel that she had to mark her territory—an idea that she found "sweet and repulsive." But she did possess some fears. She explained she had a pattern of befriending gay men who were single. Once they "grew up" and found a boyfriend, she was left alone. I said that was my experience with straight women. They were only friends with gay men to pass the time. What they truly wanted was a straight man to help them bring unneeded kids in the world.

"I'll take a risk with you," she said. "You're cute and desperate."

"I'll take a risk with you," I said. "You're charming and more desperate."

"We were made for each other," she said.

*

I've always had very few male friends in my life—straight or gay. I wish I could pass the buck and say that my lack of connection with heterosexual men comes from their homophobia. But that would not be true. I find that straight men are pretty accepting of gay people, at least in the circles I travel. And if their girlfriend likes you, they go along with it with even more gusto; sometimes they are even flirty. They have a sense of pride: It shows the world how sensitive they are.

I've always found young heterosexual women to be much more homophobic. They don't know what to do with you; you're not their daddy and if you don't encourage sentimentality, you're not their best friend. There is no place for you in their life.

Conversely, gay men can be horribly sexist. They tell women they are beautiful for a number of reasons, not always because they are. To tell a woman she is beautiful means you are looking; it means you have the power of the (heterosexual) male gaze. It makes you feel masculine in a way you might not normally.

Also, having been bullied when I was young, I lost touch with my own body. I still sometimes feel like my mind and body are unconnected. The body is always something I'm willing to sacrifice. Sometimes it's just too heavy. Through a friendship with a beautiful woman, I can mistake myself as good-looking. I can say to myself: *Of course I'm attractive. There's no way she'd spend time with someone unattractive. Would she?*

*

After our group meetings, Olive and I made fun of the incest survivors. We were assholes. We were proud that we refused to sentimentalize our abuse. We could tolerate the ones who were raped—especially if it was done by a stranger. "But those incest victims," Olive said. "They are really whiny. And some of them are ugly as hell. No one would touch them except a bored family member."

"Some of them do look really messed up. You can tell the stress has wreaked havoc on their skin," I said.

"Rape ruins your complexion," she said. "That's something people really need to start talking about."

Of course, we made sure no one else heard us talking about them—the "freaks," we said. We always wondered if they were jealous of us. How could they not be? We were stylish. We took out as much student loan money as we could to buy new clothes and eat at expensive restaurants. Some of the people in the group said they were too depressed to take care of themselves. One said that she stopped cleaning her dishes. She let her dog lick the bowl. Olive and I looked at one another. We could barely control ourselves from laughing. We couldn't remember. Was she the one who made the cupcakes for the meeting?

*

Before I came out as gay, my romantic experiences with women always predictably flopped. My prom date was my best friend Alicia, who wore a tuxedo jacket/miniskirt combo to the dance and two weeks later came out as a lesbian. My freshman year of college I tried to date a woman and when things turned sexual, we became unnaturally silent and then one of us started crying about something that didn't matter. The other finally said, "I know what will make you feel better! An ice cream drink." Which got us out of the bedroom and into a public place where we could just talk and, sure enough, we soon felt better.

For the longest time, my sexual experiences with men weren't much different, except that I usually became aroused, and wanted to make it through to the end, as long as the end was near. I have no regrets about anything I did. Often during sex I saw myself as an eccentric anthropologist, accumulating data for later projects, observing everything, including myself, with a sweet, dumb, persistent detachment.

"Have you ever kissed a woman?" Olive once asked me over the phone.

This is what I said: "In junior high, I went to a dance with a girl. I was nervous. Not about her. But her brothers. They were Greek and protective and mean. At the dance, I tried to kiss her and she pushed me away. She laughed, 'I know you're gay. That's why my brothers let me go with you.'

And then she stepped forward and said, 'Come dance with me.' And I did."

Olive said, "If I was sitting right next to you now, I'd lean over and kiss you. You're so sweet. You're like a little pet."

*

As an undergraduate, I never liked going home for the summer. I would see the person who did stuff to me when I was young. Olive never knew how scared I was. I knew what she would say. She would say: No, don't go back there. Stay with my grandparents and me.

I was relieved and oddly sad that she said that. It was the only time in my life that I wanted to marry a woman. I wanted to have that security. Sometimes to ask for certain things you need to have a contract and a ring.

It is now more than twenty years since Olive and I have been friends. A lot has changed since the '90s. When marriage became a possibility in New York, I got hitched. My husband is a cute, intelligent man named Phil.

We didn't waste any time putting rings on each other's fingers. We bought them at Walmart ($15 apiece!) and then raced down to city hall. The rings didn't fit well. Two days after the marriage, the ring flew off my finger and got stuck in a Wegman's cashier conveyor belt.

I don't know if Olive ever got married. If so, I hope they end up getting a divorce. I'm not a mean person. I do want it to be an amiable separation.

*

I always wondered, when Olive and I were seen in public, did people assume we were dating? On our way to marriage?

More than a few times, she said, "People might think you're fucking me. Isn't that weird?"

Was she shocked and disappointed that someone would assume she was with me?

She was the kind of person who looked different from every angle. From some, she looked voluptuous and sexy; others, frumpy; and in a few, anorexic. I think she was conscious of that fact. She was always moving. Trying to find her best side. Once I said to her: "You're so jittery. As if you're always trying to get away from someone staring at you."

"There's probably some truth to that," she said. "Remember we did meet in a sexual abuse support group."

*

Once at the support group, a woman told everyone about her father who snuck into her room and touched her during the middle of the night with a kitchen utensil. Olive was biting her lip to keep from laughing.

The woman was talking about how, for a number of reasons, she hadn't told anyone about the abuse. There were simply too many other tragedies for her to deal with over the years. One of her brothers lost a leg in a freak boating accident. Her mother had died. Her grandmother was sick. A sister tried to kill herself. I don't know if I've ever met someone who's suffered more heartbreak. You would have thought she asked for it. God's punishment.

The woman went home for the summers. Whoever was left of her family would pick her up at the airport. Her father would always go to hug her. She never knew how long the embrace should last.

"Until it feels unnatural," Olive said.

"My father was the first and last man to ever touch me. I don't know what natural is," she said.

"Here," Olive said. She was pointing at me. "Try him out. He's gay. He's practically neutered." Olive laughed. I didn't get the joke. No one else seemed to either.

The woman approached me and said, "May I have a hug?"

I stood. I put my arms around her.

She slapped me across the face. It hurt.

Olive asked her why she slapped me. "I don't know," she said. "The feeling came over me and I just went with it."

*

Now I am an associate professor at a state university in an exceptionally dull rural area. But I do actually like my job. I was hired to teach creative nonfiction, more specifically, memoir. There is one word that I ban on the first day of class: *courageous.*

I know that if I don't do that my students will use the word endlessly. We'll discuss an essay about bulimia. They'll say: Courageous. We'll discuss an essay about divorce. They'll say: Courageous. We'll discuss an essay about a bad boyfriend. They'll say: Courageous.

I try to remember if Olive ever used the word *courageous* when someone talked about their sexual abuse. I think she did what I do now with my creative nonfiction students when I'm tired.

After they finish, I smile and then look away and say, "Next."

*

I always anticipate people leaving me.

When I was friends with Olive, I found myself taking a number of women's studies classes. I liked to pretend to myself that I was interested in the lives of the marginalized, such as people of color, women, and gays and lesbians.

But that wasn't the truth.

This was the truth: I was looking for someone who would turn out to be an eventual replacement for Olive. The women who took the classes were always more complicated. They knew that there was something else out there. They were suspicious.

I always made sure that I came out as gay in those classes.

I also figured that if I came out, my liberal professors would remember me, look at me fondly, and excuse my spotty attendance, incomplete papers.

It worked. In one of my classes, I completed less than two-thirds of the weekly written assignments and I still received a solid A and a personal note telling me that I made phenomenal contributions to her class. During the first week, I said, "I'm gay. And men—gay and straight—need to fight for the equality of women and men in the world."

That was all I said for the entire semester. I never did any of the readings. My rationale at the time: Feminism is common sense. Why study something I already know in my heart?

*

You fucking bitch. Those were the first words that came out of my mouth when Olive told me she met a man she wanted to date: You fucking bitch.

She didn't tell me about their first date; she didn't think it was important. But now she'd discovered she might like him. This was a brief rundown of his most significant characteristics: He was a chemical engineer and talked about the elements on the periodic table as if they were close personal friends. He was a man who asked you questions. Always a rarity. He was a bit agoraphobic. He was forty-five and had no wrinkles. She said it was almost eerie. They made jokes that some big business was going to kidnap him and steal his skin to create an anti-wrinkle formula, making a billion dollars off the product. She loved to watch him eat. He did it with dignity. (I scarfed down my food.) His name was Tim. "He's obsessed with movies, just like you," she said.

She brought me along on their third date. She demanded that I call him on the phone. I thought it would look odd. She didn't care. She wanted me to hear the sound of his voice. "The quality of someone's voice reveals the texture of their soul," she said.

He sounded like a good guy, someone who could easily win her heart and take her away from me. I didn't know what to say to him. I told him my obsession with movie reviews. Every Friday morning, I would wake up and immediately race down to the nearest convenience store and purchase all the local and national newspapers, clipping out the reviews and reading them over and over again, anticipating what I would be seeing over the next week. I had done that for as long as I could remember.

"I'm not that into movies," Tim said.

"Olive said you were really into them."

"It was a little white lie," he said. I couldn't tell if he was lying. Maybe he was trying to build a phony secret with me, so I would approve of him.

"So I win?"

There was a long silence.

"Win what?" he said. "I didn't know we were competing."

Martin Scorsese's *Cape Fear* had just been released, and I asked if he approved.

I described the movie. He admitted that he loved thrillers, especially the violent and gritty ones. I had read that one of the subplots involved a weird, perverse relationship between a predatory male and an underage girl.

"How will that make Olive feel?" Tim asked.

"She won't care," I said. "Just make it clear to her that it was your choice. What matters to her more than anything is pleasing the other person."

*

When Tim came to pick us up to see *Cape Fear,* he said to me, "I didn't think you'd end up coming with."

"Today is the night I spend with Olive," I said. "Gay men aren't always sashaying around, making empty promises." Men fall harder for women who are in demand. I was being a jerk for Olive. Later I'd tell her she owed me. My rudeness was an act of generosity.

"Friday night is Steve's night with me. He's generous in sharing it with you," Olive said.

Tim said to me, "Olive says how amazing you are. All the time. It makes me jealous. In a good way. Maybe one day she'll talk about me the way she talks about you."

I didn't know what to say.

"It's cool you met at that group," he said. "It's especially cool that you go. Being a man and all. I imagine it must be difficult for a man to be there. Do many go to things like that?"

"I don't know," I said. "It's the first and only support group I attend. If I become a connoisseur of them, I'll tell you what one has the best male-female ratio. Maybe if you and Olive don't work out, it can be a new pickup joint."

*

Things didn't turn out well at *Cape Fear.* After the first two violent, extremely bloody scenes, containing the threat of rape, Olive excused herself. I didn't stop her. I needed there to be something wrong.

"What's up?" Tim whispered to me in the theatre.

"Let me go check," I said.

I left him and found her in the lobby, her head in her hands.

"Sorry," I said, putting my arm around her. "I didn't think that movie was the right choice."

"Then why did you take me?"

"Tim took you. I warned him about the movie. Told him you'd have a difficult time with it."

And then I started to make up lies. I told her Tim thought she needed to toughen up and transcend what happened, and he was just the man to do it. I told her that he thought watching the images could help her recover. I told her that he wanted her to have sympathy for her abuser.

"What a creep," she said. "Let's go."

"Where?"

"Away," she said. "Just you and me."

"OK," I said, "if that's how you want it."

*

Within a week, Olive found out everything. Tim begged her to meet him for coffee. She liked him, so she went. How could she not? He was a good man. He could love her in the right way.

Later she confronted me. I confessed my plot.

"But why?" she asked me before our weekly group meeting.

"I needed something."

She looked at me confused: "You needed me?"

"Not exactly," I said.

She said she would forgive me if I agreed to find a new sexual abuse support group and never speak to her again.

I said, "How about we remain friends and you just never forgive me?"

"No," she said.

*

I did what she asked of me, against my own desire. From time to time, I thought about showing up at the group, seeing if enough time had elapsed, if we could put the past behind us and resume our relationship. Once I even made it as far as the building, but couldn't bring myself to enter, and instead I circled around the premises, careful not to be seen by any of the people coming in and out. I couldn't bring myself to go in. Only once I saw her leave. I must admit: I felt the urge to tackle her. Not to hurt her. But just to stop her dead in her tracks and say, "Please listen. I have something to say." Sometimes you have to be a little forceful with people to get heard.

I feared she would say it was unethical, almost like a violation.

She said no, and I had to listen. Her no meant no. There was no other way to read it. At least that's what I needed to convince myself of.

Here is a confession: Like most men, I couldn't accept her no for the longest time. There was a part of me that always wanted to read her no as a timid, shy come-on, a closeted yes, a yes waiting to become something else, a potential thank you for not accepting no as no.

I cannot tell you the number of times I wanted to enter that building.

In a way, I felt like I had a right. In some ways, I still do.

By accepting Olive's forgiveness, by not coming to group, by ending the friendship, by struggling with my own desires, I realized a simple truth: I was, indeed, a man.

Inside

They closed off the streets for the horses. Everyone in Salt Lake City seemed to be eating lime Jell-O. No hot dogs or Coca-Cola or junk food in sight. My partner was nervously clutching a convenience store pimento cheese sandwich. He hated crowds. He wasn't that fond of people except for me and only when I behaved myself. I tried to cheer him up, pointing to my favorite Pioneer Day float: a man dressed in overalls holding his wife's hand who stood inside a huge jelly jar. You could tell the cap was screwed on especially tight. It made me nervous. How could anyone breathe inside a jelly jar? Draped alongside the platform was a sign that said: PRESERVE MORMON CULTURE. I kept half-expecting the man and woman to fall over from a lack of oxygen—they looked like lightning bugs some kid had caught—but they kept waving, unbothered that they were trapped, unable to even fully move their arms.

I imagined bolting from the crowd, leaping on top of the lid, prying my way in, and then yelling at them to "Hurry! Take my hand!" so I could help them get out.

Phil tapped my shoulder, and said that he desperately needed a Mountain Dew or any conceivable caffeinated beverage. Those were the words he used: "caffeinated beverage."

"Shut up," I said.

"But I'm thirsty. I need coldness. I need caffeine." It was 101 degrees outside. We had been trapped inside my studio for a week now. Phil, who sometimes refers to himself as a "pseudo-agoraphobic," didn't like going outside, especially in this heat, and I didn't own a car. I didn't even know how to drive.

My panic about driving was something I was working on. It sprang, I guess, from my memories of riding around with my mother in our old green Datsun. The car was the color of the cartoon character Gumby, and my mother would constantly scream at any driver who dared even to come near us on the road. "Get off my tail, asswipe!" "Move out of the way, Fatass!" "Use a goddamned turn signal, you old blue-haired bitch!" The thought of any other car either in front of us, beside us, or behind us drove my mother into a near-homicidal rage. The only time she seemed to be happy behind the wheel of an automobile was when we were sitting with the engine off in our own garage, and even then, I some-times imagined, she was probably mad at the walls. Now, I couldn't drive—in my mind, even as an adult, I would always be the other driver my mother was yelling at: slow-ass or dumbass or asswipe. My psychiatrist told me it was time to conquer my fear, so he prescribed me anti-anxiety pills and waived my appointment fees, and twisted my arm so I could take driver's ed. I ended up in the backseat of a Volvo with two sixteen-year-old slutty girls, watching an uptight Mor-mon boy cower as our instructor berated him for messing up a three-point turn. The teacher's yelling made me so nervous I distracted myself by staring at the girls' breasts. They didn't seem to mind.

Phil said, "I really am thirsty."

"I didn't think you were lying," I said.

"You're always fussin' at me," he said. You could tell he was from the South. He sometimes used dumb words like "fussin'" or "holler" or even really outdated ones like "consideration." He nearly had a doctorate in English and he still sometimes preferred to sound like the Beverly Hillbillies.

"I need a Mountain Dew or a Mello Yello," he said.

I grabbed his arm and told him to fuck off. "Don't you get it?" I said. "We're in Utah. Show some respect. You don't say the names of caffeinated beverages aloud at a Mormon festival. It's practically blasphemy, like praying aloud to an Aztec god in the middle of the Vatican."

"It's 150 degrees. I'm dehydrated, you asshole," he said, gesturing toward a float for the LDS Hospital. A beautiful woman in a nightgown, lying in her hospital bed, was waving to the crowds. She looked like a high school beauty queen, and was obviously not sick at all. An IV was scotch-taped to her arm. "That'll be me in a minute, if I don't get something to drink," said Phil.

Someone next to me said that the woman in the hospital gown was the best damn Ashtanga yoga instructor in the city.

"What an actress," I whispered to Phil.

"Well, when they shove me in a hospital bed for dehydration, I won't be waving. Not to you, anyway. It's hard to fake happiness when you don't feel it," he said.

There was no way I was going to fetch him a caffeinated beverage from the convenience store down the block.

He knew I found Mormon fathers attractive. I loved the way they obeyed their wives. They possessed a weakness I found irresistible. Phil never seemed to scope the crowds for cute guys. Once I asked him why that was so. He said, I dunno, and that I wasn't that bad.

"Not perfect," he said, "but not too bad. At least on most days."

I thought I knew what his real mission was. He wanted to trap me in a jelly jar, put the lid on so tight that you'd have to slam the jar hard on the floor to get me out. And even then, there'd be great risk to my well-being. The cracked glass would disfigure my face, or I'd end up with a shattered leg. No one would want to be with me except Phil. Once I confessed this nightmare to him. "Hey," he said, "anytime you want to leave, there's the door." And then he smiled. "But you know the old joke. When is a door not a door? When it's ajar."

"You're not getting a caffeinated beverage," I said.

Phil's face was all red and sweaty. I was embarrassed. Mormons were always well-showered.

Phil knew I was stuck with him.

"I need to sit down," he said.

"But we're going to miss a float."

"I need to sit down," he repeated. He sat down. A kid immediately stepped on his hand. Phil winced.

"I want to go look at the horse and buggy up close," I said.

"Don't leave me," he said. "I'll be abducted, like Elizabeth Smart."

"I want to see the animals," I said. I knew he'd have to let me go, because Phil was obsessed by animals and liked when I was charmed by four-legged things. Once we had a pet rabbit. I let it run around my apartment and poop everywhere. Phil told me that when he gets sick of me, he tries to recall that image and remember I'm not an entirely bad person. "Anyone who lets their bunny shit all over the place can't be too bad," he says.

I started to walk toward the horse and buggy; Phil lagged behind. I felt bad so I turned away from the parade and marched toward the restaurants. "Let's make sure we go somewhere that has a patio," I said.

"It's so hot outside," he said.

That was something else I didn't like about Phil. He liked air-conditioning. My claustrophobia increased when we turned it on. I hated having all the windows shut; it drove me crazy.

We ended up at a Chinese restaurant called Chang's. Phil said, "You can tell this place has good food."

"Why do you think that?"

"The air-conditioning is on. That's always a good sign."

We were seated in the far corner of the restaurant. It was pretty crowded. As soon as we sat down, two men seated near the entrance started speaking loudly. I tried to ignore them, scoping out the buffet. One of the men had a handlebar mustache; the other one wore a salmon-colored shirt. I could tell Phil was watching them too. Their conversation was loud and intense.

We approached the buffet. The two men started yelling even louder. One of the men stood, then the other did. Finally the mustached man hammered one of his fists on the table. Suddenly it was a bad saloon scene from *Gunsmoke*. Shootout at the Chinese All-You-Can-Eat Buffet. The other man started shrieking "Motherfucker! Motherfucker!" which caused the mustached man to grab the table by its legs; he pushed the table as hard as he could, knocking the shrieking man to the ground. Phil looked at me and said, "Let's go."

I didn't know what to do. I was hungry.

People started to get up. That didn't cause the men to stop. The shrieking man sprang to his feet from the floor and waved his fists, shrieking even louder. "Motherfucker! Motherfucker! I'll cut you! Motherfucker!" We didn't see a knife, but that didn't stop us from scurrying toward the door. For some reason, I stopped dead in my tracks several feet later. Phil was already past me. Phil often said that once I learned how to drive, I'd be the driver who rubbernecked at automobile accidents, causing one myself. I imagined the mustached man shoving the shrieking man so hard into the wall that he'd smash right through, falling in front of several pedestrians on the sidewalk like Slim Pickens crashing through a plate glass window in some 1950s western.

Phil grabbed my arm. At first, I pulled back, as if I was going to stay. The men both simultaneously looked up at me, almost as though they were going to ask Phil and I to join in, but before they could say or do anything, I was out the door, trying to remember why I allowed myself to linger in such a potentially bad situation.

"Let's go home," Phil said. "If we'd stayed long enough to get the fortune cookie, you know it'd say this is not a good day to leave the apartment."

I shrugged. "Stop!" somebody cried from behind us. Phil and I both prepared to bolt, sensing that, somehow or other, fate was pulling us inevitably back toward a barroom brawl, armed combat, and a good old-fashioned, all-you-can-eat beating. But the voice was too high, too piercing, even for the shrieking man. "Stop! Hey!!! Stop!!!" We stopped. It was my best friend's sister. Even under these circumstances, I was only marginally surprised to see her. Though Salt Lake claimed to be a city, it always seemed like a small town, and everybody always kept running into everybody else.

It was too hot for a pregnant woman to be outside. My best friend's sister reeked of vodka.

"Hello. Have you been drinking?" Phil said, staring at her stomach.

"Are you judging me?" she said. "Are . . . you . . . judging . . . me? My doctor said I could have one drink a day. It won't hurt the baby." She opened her purse, looked in it intensely for a minute as though confirming the diagnosis with an obstetrician hidden behind her tampons. Then she stood up razor-straight. She held out her hand. "I'm Flo, by the way. Pleased to meet you."

"Uhhhm, Phil. Steve's told me a lot about you?" It was a question. Phil could be a good liar, and I should know, so it's always clear whenever he doesn't care enough to hide an insincerity. It was obvious to everyone that Phil had never heard of Flo before in his life. I could tell that Phil wasn't charmed by Flo like I was. If she'd charmed him, he'd have lied much more believably, as a courtesy. As for me, sure, I couldn't ignore the image of the baby inside Flo's body trying to dodge the alcohol entering her bloodstream. I pictured the baby kicking her stomach, upset that it couldn't just be left the hell alone. But I liked Flo. I did.

She took a half-filled bottle out of her purse. "Wanna join me?" she said.

Phil shook his head. He glared at me with a "Can we fucking go home now" look.

"It's mean to let a lady drink alone," she said.

I grabbed the bottle from her and chugged some vodka.

"How did you get here?" I asked. Flo lived pretty far from the restaurant.

"I drove, of course," she said. "Need a ride?"

"Thank you," I said.

Phil was not happy. But he was also too tired to walk.

On the way to my apartment, Flo changed lanes six times in two minutes. Phil cringed every time. We passed a construction site. Flo swerved, extremely close to the orange-and-white traffic barriers, and so wildly that she nearly ended up going in the wrong direction on the opposite side of the road. I was only obliquely conscious of the whole thing, much more interested in concentrating on Flo's anger at the man she was having an affair with. Flo talked more than a mile a minute, just like she drove.

"I know he's only nineteen," Flo said, "but don't you think he should have sprung for the motel room? It really does say a lot about his upbringing. The whole thing made me miss my husband. I know when he fucks women behind my back, he pays for the room. I know, I've seen the receipts."

"Jesus God Almighty," groaned Phil.

I loved Flo. Everything she said made sense to me.

There were wads of pastel wrapping paper and boxes of baby presents all over the car. "My aunt just threw me a shower," said Flo. "Most of the presents suck."

The car swerved into the parking lot of our apartment complex. Flo asked if we wanted to come drink at the Twilight Lounge with her.

Phil looked incredulous. "Uhhh, Steve . . ." he muttered.

"Oh, don't worry," I said. "I've got plenty of money. I'll buy, cheapskate."

"Oh, no," laughed Flo. "Drinks are on me."

"Uhhh, no, Steve," said Phil. "I've got that phone call. You know the phone call I'm expecting. That we're expecting. The phone call that you need to be there for. Inside."

"Phone call?" I said. "What phone call?"

"Are you working for the FBI?" Flo asked. "If so, you're right; the phone call can't wait. Otherwise keep your ass in my car and let's go party." She turned on the radio.

Phil raised his voice above the music. "No. Steve's got to get this phone call." He started to open the car door. "Oh, and, by the way, Flo"—he bit down on the name—"it's not from the FBI. It's from a friend. He's dying." Phil paused, leaning back into the car. "Of fetal alcohol syndrome." He grinned weirdly, then trudged off toward the apartment complex.

"I should go talk to him before we take off."

"He's a pill," Flo said. "So cranky. You'd think he was the one who was pregnant."

"Just give me five minutes," I said.

I went inside and Phil was standing in the center of the studio, his arms crossed. "She's drunk," he said.

I just stood there.

"I used to drink," he said. "A lot. I know drunks. Some can function and some of them are train wrecks. Flo is like a plane that's crashed into a train that's run over a cat and crashed into a lake. You're not going back out with her."

"Fuck you," I said. "Don't be so controlling. I won't stay here with you and sweat to death in this studio. I need to get out."

"That woman has problems."

"She's fun," I said.

"She has a baby," he said.

"Well, yeah," I said, "that's one strike. But I like her. I do. You need to live in the moment for once."

"There's other moments," Phil said, "than just the most dramatic ones."

"I'm leaving," I said.

"Kiss me first," he said.

I kissed him.

"Come back soon," he said.

I left.

Flo revved up the car. I got in. Off we went. After she blew through the second stop sign I started to get nervous. "Flo, be careful."

"Wanna hear about my dream?" she said. "I know you don't. But I'm going to tell you anyway. I'm drunk. Drunk people have a right to blabber. I dreamt that I was bobbing inside a Boone's Farm strawberry wine bottle. If that wasn't bad enough, my baby was floating in the same bottle with me. Sometimes it's like we're just having fun, splashing around, like in the pool, and sometimes it's like we're both treading water, trying to stay afloat, too tired to even move toward one another."

I didn't know what to say so I kept my mouth shut.

Flo got quiet for a minute.

"Steve?" she said, turning down the radio.

"Yeah, Flo?" I said.

"I didn't really dream that." She sat still for a minute, just driving. Then she laughed, but this time it was barely a noise at all. "Sometimes, though, I feel like I am floating. That we're floating. I know this is wrong. That it's all wrong. That everything's wrong. But still . . ."

Flo pulled up into the parking lot of the Twilight Lounge. We walked into the bar where I bought her a dry Cape Cod and myself a Tequila Sunrise. We guzzled those drinks; she bought another round. I thought of Phil sitting at home waiting for a phone call that was never going to come. I felt a little guilty. Not much, but a little. Flo was too drunk to go home, so I kissed her on the cheek, paid for the drinks after I bought her another, and told her I was going to walk home. I should have called a taxi for her, but I didn't.

"I'll drive you," she said as she wobbled on her barstool.

"It's fine," I said. "I need the exercise."

I lived about two miles away from the bar. Halfway home, I stepped on some shattered glass. I was afraid I'd get cut. The moonlight shone on the scattered pieces. I checked myself; I wasn't bleeding. From one angle, the reflection off the glass looked so beautiful, so sweet. I took a few steps and resumed my brisk walk, trying to clear my head before I got home.

It seemed like only a second or two later that Flo yelled to me, several feet behind me in her car: "Hey sexy, get in! Let me give you a ride home." She reached over and opened the car door. "Let me get you to a place where you can rest your weary feet!"

Safe Haven

"So aren't you going to make the offer?" It was the first thing my mother said when I picked up the phone.

I had no idea what she was talking about. "What do you mean?"

"You're actually going to make me ask."

Again, I drew a blank.

"Oh, for God's sake," she said. "Can your brother and I stay with you? We don't have anywhere else to go."

I felt stupid. They were living in coastal Mississippi, where my brother Eric had taken a job keeping books for a few family-run hotels. My mother was staying with him after she'd given up even trying to do temp work a few years back. Once she began losing her vision, she could not hold on to a job, as much because of attitude as because of disability. So she'd left Chicago, and traveled south. She hated the South. She wasn't too keen on living with my brother, either, but at least he'd made the invite. Now their new Mississippi home was a disaster area, swept away in the wake of Katrina.

"You need to stay with me," I said, unsure even myself if I meant it as a question or a declaration.

"We need to stay with family." She said little else, and left me to make the plans.

*

The day they flew in, I went to pick them up from the airport. At first I told them I couldn't be there myself; I had class. This was half-true; I did have class, but, as the instructor, I could easily cancel. My mother's reply: "If so-help-me-God you make us get a cab, I'll pick up the goddamn white courtesy phone at the airport, page Mother Nature, and tell her to send Katrina back around to find you."

My brother trailed after my mother. He didn't look happy to see me. We hadn't talked for years. Things got weird when I went to college and left him with my mother in the trailer park back in Illinois. He never said so, but he resented me. You could tell that he was happy he became an accountant and had the money not only to take care of himself but our mother as well. He didn't mind the move to Mississippi. The conservative politics agreed with him, as did the offshore casinos.

"How are you?" I said.

"We're here," Eric said.

In the car, I asked them for details about how people were dealing with the hurricane. Did all their friends find people to stay with?

I noticed that my mother kept looking warily at my brother's face. It made me nervous. Could she somehow still see how unhappy he was to see me?

"My apartment is real small," I said. "It's real, real small, and it's going to be real cramped."

"We all lived together before," Eric said. "I'm sure we're used to this."

"Is it clean?" my mother said. This was strange and somehow insulting, coming from her. She was never a good housekeeper. Not that it was her fault. My father left us and she was forced to work three different jobs. No time to wax the trailer's floors and triple-polish the light fixtures, I guess. I'd be lucky if she'd swept the cobwebs down by allergy season.

"Yes and no," I said.

"What an answer," Eric said. "Just say it's not clean. No wonder you went to grad school—'yes and no,' everything's relative, blah, blah, blah. They don't let you flit by with that shit when you get a real job."

"Get along, dummies," my mother said. "It doesn't matter if it's clean. That's the good thing about going blind. Who cares what it looks like? All that matters is nothing bad can touch me."

Over dinner, we all drank a bottle of wine. It felt odd. Growing up in a trailer park, we never touched alcohol. It was something that set us apart from the rest of the poor families. Or so we needed to believe.

Now we were all drinking together.

The conversation hit a particularly uncomfortable lull, which was pretty amazing, since we weren't talking that much to begin with.

"How bad do you think things are going to get?" I said.

My mother reached over and pinched my hand. It didn't hurt much. But I felt embarrassed. I knew I had said something stupid.

She changed the subject. She told us that ever since she lost most of her sight, local people, particularly older women, sometimes treated her like a prophet, an oracle. They would come up to her in restaurants or even stop her in the middle of the street. They would ask her the most personal question. It was as if she was some sort of holy person. It was the strangest thing, and a little bit scary. To strangers, she could play this role. It would last only so long as there was short, casual contact; for anyone who knew her for any length of time, the illusion vanished.

"Sometimes I like the attention," my mother said.

"You always have." My brother tapped his fork against the edge of the table.

My mother looked to me for support. "Strangely enough, I'm not going to argue with him on that point," I said. "There's a first time for everything."

"Congratulations to the both of you then," my mother said.

My mother said that she was glad that now she was nowhere near Mississippi or New Orleans. She was afraid someone might approach her and ask about a relative, friend, lover. She didn't want to have to say, "I don't know."

"Sometimes I think if someone asked, it would be better to lie," my mother said. "Is there anything more cruel to say than 'I don't know'?"

"I don't know," my brother said.

I startled myself by laughing at this, and that made my brother laugh, and then we all started to laugh as if something funny had been said. As if there was some reason we deserved a release of any sort.

*

The next morning, my mother walked into my room and stumbled over a load of laundry. "If I'm aware of how much of a pigsty this place is, it really must be pretty bad," my mother said.

I didn't say anything. It was the only way I knew to punish her.

She grabbed my hand and then forced me to open my palm. "I'm going to tell you your future," she said. "I might as well take the role I've been given. Run with it. Madame Mom, the blind marvel, knows all, sees all."

I told her to go ahead. I needed something to look forward to.

She dropped my hand. "What do you mean?"

I said nothing.

"Don't tell me you need something to look forward to. Really. Don't." She seemed stunned and a little angry. "Your family is here. We're together."

"That's one way of looking at it," I said.

*

Later that day, my brother came into my room and asked if I wanted to come outside and have a smoke. I didn't smoke. But I always liked people who did. They always seemed to have a story to tell, a problem on their minds. That was why they smoked. They needed a dumb habit, a prop, to keep them focused on something else. My brother was in junior high when he started smoking. I remember the first time I saw him outside sharing a cigarette with friends. He looked so cool. I was jealous. I was the older brother. I was supposed to be more mature, edgier.

We went outside. He offered me a cigarette. I refused and he looked disappointed.

"We didn't have to stay with you," my brother said, "I have money. We could have stayed at a hotel."

"This is a good thing," I said. "I wanted for all of us to spend time together."

"Liar," my brother said.

"Are you scared?"

"A little," he said. "I didn't want anything to happen to our house. I worked for that house."

He did work for the house. A real house. Garage, attic, shutters, two stories, the whole thing. It was weird. For the first time, I became aware how important a place to live was. It sort of embarrassed me.

"A house is a good thing," I said. It sounded stupid, but I had to say it. "Do you think I'm dumb for saying that?"

"Of course not," he said. "I was thinking the same thing. Plus, you're my older brother. You can't be too stupid, even if you are an overeducated shithead."

To our surprise, my mother walked outside. My brother dropped his cigarette and squashed it with his foot.

"I lost my vision," she said, "not my sense of smell."

And then she added: "Give me a cigarette."

"You sure?" I asked.

"It's been a long couple of days," she said. "Give me a goddamn cigarette."

*

Later that night all three of us were sitting around watching TV. We couldn't watch the news; it made us too nervous. We put on a Lifetime thriller. The plot was complicated. A woman was unknowingly married to a serial killer who'd had plastic surgery so he'd look exactly like her husband, whom he secretly killed. My mother couldn't sit still. She kept gasping, saying, "Oh my God" over and over again.

I didn't understand how the movie could affect her that much. She couldn't even see the screen.

"What's your problem?" my brother said to my mother. I felt bad. How could we deny my mother her pleasure?

"I'm watching a movie," my mother said. "It's pretty intense."

"I'm watching the movie," my brother said. "It's pretty idiotic."

My mother picked up the remote and turned the sound all the way down on the TV.

"Close your eyes," she said.

Then she turned to me and said, "You too."

"OK," I said, "they're closed." I didn't close my eyes. I wasn't going to play any of her games.

"I'm no fool," she said. "Some people even think I have mystical powers. You'd better shut those eyes."

How can you ignore the command of someone with mystical powers? I shut my eyes.

The room got so silent all of a sudden. Everything else dropped away. I got scared. If you didn't let yourself breathe, you could hear traces of the wind outside. It was a low sound, more quiet than quiet, like the last remains of an echo of someone calling for help. I started to get really scared. I didn't think it was fair to open my eyes. My mother couldn't see anything. It didn't matter if she opened her eyes. I needed to be with her. I wanted to be with her.

I reached over and held her hand. I felt stupid. A grown man holding his blind mother's hand as they're watching a silent TV with their eyes closed, the lights off. This is what my life has become. For a moment, I opened my eyes and saw my brother was holding my mother's hand too.

I tightened my grip and took a deep breath.

III

How to Survive a
Baby Shower

Before you go to any get-together, you dream about the
food. Usually, it's a good thing. But sometimes it's a nightmare. Your husband Phil can always tell when some bad
images have occupied your mind over the night. You get
cranky. Panicky. You end up yelling at him for no apparent
reason. This was what you dreamt before your friend Jackie's
baby shower: a table full of scooped-out watermelons with
tiny, plastic baby dolls inside; deviled eggs cut in the shape
of little cribs; translucent bags of crunchy snacks that say
"Ready to pop!" You saw yourself binging on the avant-garde
snacks and then rushing to the bathroom to throw them up.
That's one of the many tragedies of your psychology: You've
never been able to live in denial very long. It's what would
have made you a bad parent: You can't allow anyone to be
happy. If you're going down, you're going to take everyone
down with you.

But then your dream got worse: Everyone kept saying how
excited they were for Jackie to open the gifts. You surveyed
some of her smarter friends. She was going to get some weird

shit: the Sozo Weeblock Tinkle Tinkle Lil' Star (a weird absorbent sponge); a matching pumpkin Halloween costume for the baby and her; white baby clothes (dry clean only). One woman is giving her a canvas portrait of her own child. "Something to inspire them," she says. The punchline of the dream: You had to write the thank-you cards.

Unsurprisingly, you're the token gay male best friend at the baby shower, which is on the patio of a rundown bar named Diamonds. Of course, women brag about coercing their husbands into taking care of their babies for a few hours, which, from what you hear, is quite an impossible feat. One woman is drunk, and the baby shower hasn't even officially started. She comes up to you and introduces herself as Jill and then says, "My husband and I got into a fight. He wanted to play darts at a bar. He wanted me to miss this soiree so he could play darts. Darts!?!?"

You don't say: "He's probably with some other woman. No one plays darts anymore." It's true, darts is something the cavemen did to pass the time: whip some twig at the center of a tree. Every guy, even octogenarians, plays video games.

You offer to get her another drink, which she needs.

"That's so sweeeeet," she snorts. "You must be Jackie's gay best friend. You're nice. Gays are always nice. Are you nice?"

"No."

"Too bad," she says. "Please fetch that drink."

It seems sadistic: an expectant mother expending her energy thanking everybody. Each person secretly wants their own personalized, spontaneous exclamation of gratitude. What does she do when she opens a box and there's some raggedy-ass stuffed animal that looks like a cross between a triceratops and their mother-in-law? Gratitude is a hard thing to fake. Hit the wrong note and you sound like you're screeching.

You want to say that you don't know how Jackie is going to do it. But Jackie has endless energy. She's someone who was born to be a mother. She wants to be a mother. Now. Fifteen years since graduate school. The bar-hopping has been over for a while.

Soon Jackie won't even remember the days of going to your favorite place, The Hole in the Wall, and you waving goodbye to her as she left with some unappealing Irish guy who worked at the post office as his main gig and made ice sculptures on the side. He created the most beautiful swans. You would have stayed with him just to hear him chiseling in another room. She would never admit why she refused to break it up: He had a daughter from a previous marriage. Her name was Gertie. Cute kid. She was always sucking on a Jolly Rancher. If you asked her for one, she balked. She didn't like to share. Which you liked. Girls are expected to give things away.

You remember when Jackie first fell in love with the kid. She called you up on the phone and bragged that Gertie gave her a Jolly Rancher. Without her even asking. It was the color (yellow) that tasted the worst. But still. Progress.

Another woman approaches you at the party. Her name is Juliet. She's holding a baby, which was supposed to be illegal at this shower—something that could get you thrown out. No babies. That's what it said in the invitations.

Juliet shoves the baby in your face. It's ugly. It's a really, really ugly baby. Yet the baby seems to have some weird sense of pride. It sticks out its tongue and rubs his feet together. Like he has one up on you. Like he's cursed any of your future happiness.

"His name is Damien," Becky says as the baby raises his hand smiling. As if he just gave you the finger. Maybe he did.

You say, "That's funny. I liked *The Omen,* too. Good flick." Then you look at the baby, concerned you might have upset him. "Really good movie," you say.

"I never saw it," Becky says. "You're a little older than me, I think. What's it about?"

You remember the scene where Damien is on a tricycle, riding around upstairs, sick of listening to his nanny order him around. He rams into her and she falls from the second floor to her death.

"A real ambitious tyke," you say. "You should check it out sometime."

*

Jackie is older than some women who have children. She knew some nasty people would say it was a ridiculous age to do such a thing, and that it wasn't fair to the child. It didn't take much to conjure up the nasty image: a pimply faced teenager with a slight limp gripping the back of Jackie's wheelchair, adjusting the oxygen tank, rolling her down the street as she coughs and wheezes. Which you decide isn't that bad of a future. There's always worse. Damien would roll her into traffic, right in front of a semi. Just for the hell of it.

In their seventies and still in good health, Jackie's parents loved that she was having a baby. You secretly wanted them to withhold their support. It wasn't fair that she was going to leave you for a baby. Why couldn't Jackie just have another lame boyfriend? The last was obsessed with Hungry, Hungry Hippos. No joke. You and Jackie and the Hungry, Hungry Hippos world-class champion would sit around a card table, smashing the rotund creatures' fat necks, hoping that they would gobble up some marbles real quick.

It was after this guy that she decided to have a baby. It took time. But she did it.

"I know it's what I want," she said. The way she said it made you want to cry. You weren't sure why. But you wanted to take her in your arms and say, "Everything's going to be OK." Maybe that affirmation wasn't even meant for her.

"If you see me do it," she said, "you might want to get one of your own."

Jackie's sister, Marcia, has triplets. She likes two of them. Can't stand the youngest. Despises him. "If I was Meryl Streep in *Sophie's Choice*, I wouldn't even need to think twice about the one that I'd give up," she always says.

Being a veteran, Marcia's least favorite thing about baby showers are the games. She likes when there's arts and crafts though. She likes to paint rocks bright colors and write messages on them.

She gives you a misshapen rock. "This one is a little weird, don't you think?"

"I've never seen a rock that looks like that before," you say.

"That's what I like about it. It looks damaged. Like you threw it at your husband after he pissed you off and somehow it got dented," she says. "But you're right. Let's play it safe. This is my *sister's* baby shower after all."

She hands you a different rock. It looks like a normal rock. Very unassuming. Very rock-like. "Do this one. You're gay. Pretend you're Keith Haring. Make it a happy rock."

"What artist are you going to be?"

"Who would I be? *Who would I be?*" she says. "I'm an original, bitch."

*

Five minutes later. "You first." You show her your rock bespectacled in peacock-blue paint. You're proud of your creation. You think you captured the outline of a one-eared Van Gogh.

"Is that supposed to be a *human* figure?" she asks. "It looks more like the Hamburglar."

She shows you her rock. All it has is one word on it. It says: Tits. T. I. T. S. Instead of a dot on the I, there is a star.

"That's art," you say.

"You better believe it."

After you're done admiring your artwork, you turn and see a pair of gay men, holding hands, one of them carrying a baby in his arms. You do a double take, which reveals your age. It always surprises you when you see *public* gay male affection. Once in the back of your classroom, one of the students caressed the back of his boyfriend's neck. You felt threatened, even though you had a husband and, at times, are an activist. But you weren't going to have it. Not in your classroom. After class, you went up to them and snapped: "No slutting around in my class." You glanced at one of their backpacks. There was an out, loud, and proud pin. Shit. Activists.

Immediately you feared they'd complain and you would lose your job. "I was joking," you said. "Good to be visible. Out there. Out in the open. In my classroom, too. Proud of you. Really proud. Your parents must have raised you well. Tell them they have my congratulations!" That's one thing you've learned in life: When you do something wrong, make it a comic spectacle. Camp it up.

Now middle-aged, and after twenty or more years together, you barely remember any times you touched your husband publicly, even in New York City when you were seeing *Hedwig and the Angry Inch,* sitting in the midst of crowds of drag queens.

Here, at this party, the gay men waltz in with all the confidence in the world. "Don't be nervous," Marcia says. "Worse comes to worst, we can stone them to death."

The gay men see you and rush over. One is wearing overalls. Somehow he looks classy. The other looks like he's wearing makeup. You wonder if he's unsuccessfully trying to cover up what appears to be a cold sore on his bottom lip. All you can think: If that promiscuous man has a child, then why shouldn't I? Your next thought: You're a horrible person. You sound more right-wing than your father.

"You're Steve, right? We heard about you," says Cold Sore. "We're Jackie's other gay best friends."

"We're the spare," Overalls says.

Cold Sore says, "Jackie really cares about you. You know that. She would do anything for you." Like you need his affirmation.

"Is this your baby?" you say.

"Rental," Cold Sore says.

"You chose a really cute one," you say. "Must have charged you above market price."

Marcia is getting bored with all the queer niceties. She thought you were going to be her wingman this afternoon.

"Traitor," she says under her breath and walks away.

*

Overalls says, "Do you want to hold Chuck?" You didn't expect their baby to be named Chuck. Chuck is the name of an air-conditioner repairman or an Instacart shopper or the winner of a hot-dog-eating contest. Maybe they thought giving him a butch name would toughen him up. He wouldn't lead the life of a homosexual.

"Maybe later," you say. "I've never held a baby before. I'm scared."

Cold Sore speaks: "Jackie said you were thinking of having a child." You don't tell him the truth. Once someone said to your husband, "You would make an excellent father," and then said to you, "You'd be a great pushy stage mom." It was something you privately aspired to. You liked the idea of forcing your child to appear in some overproduced Broadway musical where the cast members zip around on stage in roller skates, belting out love songs while dressed in obnoxious glittery swimsuits.

But it's never happened. When you and your husband go to bed, you have a trio of stuffed animals that you play with. You have imaginary backstories for them. One is called Mr. Pokey, a stuffed bear, who used to hang out with Sammy Davis Jr. and the rest of the Rat Pack. Another is a stuffed bunny named Bunny Bunny who has cameos in a lot of '80s movies such as *The Breakfast Club* and *Octopussy*. The other is Bucky, a buckhorn, who was abandoned by his parents. He's a troublemaker, but he's ultimately vulnerable, and complex for a stuffed animal. Sometimes he slips and calls you Daddy.

When Jackie first became pregnant, it seemed that each week, things got worse in your life. During the fourth week, you ripped your favorite paisley tie. During the sixth, someone stole your wallet with a lotto card inside that you never cashed. It was worth $250. During the thirteenth, a bird almost shit on your head. During the sixteenth, the worst happened: You went home to see your mother. She's in a dementia ward. She calls you Sunny. You have no idea why. But you find it charming. In fact, when Jackie asks you if you have any idea for a name of the baby, you joke, "Sunny." It's an in-joke with yourself.

"How about Sebastian?" she says.

"No. It sounds like a pirate. You might as well call it Bluebeard." You know you don't make any sense, but you don't care. Throwing non sequiturs at an upcoming mother is a good thing. Babies don't make sense. You're going to have to go with the flow sometimes. You're teaching her a good thing.

Or maybe you just wanted to irritate her. She promised that she would go with you to see your mother. Now she couldn't. The airlines wouldn't let her fly even if she wanted to.

The dementia ward was sort of depressing. Your mother ran up to you and she held your head in her hands and then you started to smell something funny. It was shit. There was shit on her hands. Now there was shit on your face. You used her bathroom to wash yourself off and then you realized you needed to clean her up. She did it for you all those years and you bet you weren't easy. First off, you were a fat baby. A really, really fat baby. Now you're a fat adult. Nothing much has changed.

The nurse comes into the room and you tell her that you'll clean up your mother, and she says, "You sure? We have people for that."

She looks at your mother, and asks, "Is that all right with you?" Your mother nods, and the nurse says, "OK then." You figure out the shower is at the end of the hallway. You reach to hold your mother's hand and then you realize she still has shit on them. You don't care, at the same time, you do, and you hold her hand tightly. She tries to escape your grip, but you don't let her. You make it to the bathroom door. You hold the door open for her, and you swear to yourself to remember to clean the knob. There's shit there, too. At first, you don't notice the stream of pee coming from beneath her nightgown, and once you do, you think, "Fuck it, she's doing nothing wrong, she's a baby, babies make mistakes."

*

Someone announces why Jackie isn't there: car accident. Everything's OK. It's minor. Someone just backed into her car. Again, everything's OK. It'll be a half an hour though. You imagine Jackie waddling into the baby shower with her new T-shirt that says, "DON'T TOUCH MY STOMACH, BITCHES!," which isn't meant humorously. Which you love her for. You imagine her naked in front of her full-length bedroom mirror, gloating to herself as she holds her belly: "This is all mine." Perhaps that's the most enviable thing about having a child: For some time, it's all yours.

Someone asks if they can have a volunteer to go pick up ice, some more alcohol, and Gino's pizza rolls. Fortunately, your car is in the shop. Jill raises her hand and says, "I'm bored. I'll go." Everyone looks relieved.

Jill says, "But I need help carrying stuff. My arthritis has been acting up since I made those deviled eggs."

She looks at you and says, "You're a man. Help me carry things."

In the car, you notice that Jill is wearing a plastic wedding ring, something you'd buy in those little machines where you turn the knob and you automatically receive something. She grips the wheel and says, "This isn't my real wedding ring. I don't wear the real one anymore. For a number of reasons."

She parks outside Billy Ray's Liquor Store and takes out a thermos from the glove compartment and says, "Have a drink with me, my new friend. My new childless friend." Behind her seat, there's two plastic wine glasses—she gives you the one with the broken stem.

"What are you pouring me?"

"What else," she says. "Tequila Sunrise. Extra grenadine. And also, if you want, a line of coke."

She immediately starts laughing, which calms you down. You assume she's joking. At the same time, she is a mess. You imagine her accidentally dumping some of the white powder in the fake mimosas at the shower, causing a few unsuspecting victims to start crank calling the PTA Mother of the Year, threatening to call Child Protective Services on her.

"Teasing," Jill says, rolling up her window. "Let's get a couple of six packs of Boone's Strawberry Wine Coolers." She seems totally sadder. *Was* she joking?

Before you get out, she grabs your hands. "Did I tell you? I'm a part-time fortune teller." You imagine her snorting a line or two before a customer comes into her shop, which results in her making things up just to get a reaction out of people. "A heard of llamas will stampede your car in 2030." Or "You're going to be diagnosed with cancer in a few years. You'll be ready to hang yourself. But you'll find out it was a computer error. The next day you'll be shot by a criminal in a 7-11 down the block." Shit like that.

"I'm for real," she says. "I don't lie."

You don't say anything, and that doesn't stop her from touching the creases of your palms and saying, "Long life line. Sorry."

"Why sorry?"

"You're going to go through a lot of horrible things," she says. "And you won't even have kids to blame it on. But you have a lot of animals. Pet dogs."

You want her to go a step further so you can write her off as a drug-addled fraud. "And you have names for them."

You jerk your hand away. She knows.

"Your husband forgives you for not wanting a child. He forgives you for taking away something he never had."

You never told Jackie about the time you heard Phil talking to his mother after he brought you home from the psych ER. You thought he was going to tell her about having to sit in a lobby next to a teenage arsonist who lit an entire warehouse of pianos on fire. Phil couldn't stop picturing the pianos burning, the flames burrowing into the keyboards, releasing the strings, catapulting them into the air.

But this isn't what Phil was chatting about with his mother. He said to her: "Mom, Steve never wants to be a dad. It has nothing to do with being gay. He struggles with mental illness. He'd be afraid he'll mess it up."

And you've never told this to anyone, not him, not your own mother, not your friends, no one. So many secrets. They're bound to come out.

A few weeks ago, you told your playwriting students you wanted them to stop thinking in clichés. They had to create an original scene out of one of the most banal, overused scenarios in the history of theatre. They shut their eyes and you asked them to imagine visiting their mother in the hospital, holding her hand as she takes her final breaths. "Now," you asked, "what are your final words to her?" The first student says: "I love you, Mom. You made me the person—" And you cut her off. You berated her. You told her that is what everyone would say to their parent. You told her that no mother in real life would be content with such drivel. You said, "She would leave this world disappointed."

*

Inside the liquor store, the cashier, a skinny meth head, sits on a stool doing the *New York Times* crossword puzzle. Otherwise, it's all empty. Jill stops and talks to him. You're walking around the aisles, and scan the store, looking at all the dozens and dozens of bottles, thinking: *Some of these bottles could bring my happiness. Some could ruin my night. Everything is arbitrary. Surprise is possible.*

Jill is flirting with the cashier, or scoring a deal. Can't tell. You are looking at the merlots and you see one with a cartoon dragon for its label. It reminds you of the Godzilla movies you watched with your mom when you were a kid. All she wanted to see was the special effects. She stomped out of the room when any scene with a plot flashed on the screen. But seeing a duel between Mothra and Godzilla was spellbinding.

Never have you pulled a Winona Ryder before but you grab the bottle off the shelf and tuck it underneath your arm. Meth Head suffers surely from tunnel vision and you start to jog past him when he calls out, "Got you on video. I'm calling the police."

You freeze.

Meth Head's spine straightens. "My boss gives me $100 for every person I turn in," he says.

You don't care. You need this bottle. Not to drink it. But to hold it. Cradle it in your arms. Yeah, sure, you could lose your job over this dragon, which you now realize looks more like a deranged koala bear. But it's all yours. You have enough money from your shitty teaching salary to pay for this, but you shouldn't have to. It is yours. You need it. You need it so bad that you don't owe anyone an explanation. But you know Jill will take care of everything. After all, she gave you a wine glass with a broken stem. She owes you.

"I didn't leave the premises with the bottle," you say. "So it doesn't count as shoplifting yet, you dumbshit."

Jill looks at the cashier. "Yeah, you dumbshit." She gives him two $100 bills.

*

As soon as you arrive back at the party, Cold Sore doesn't waste a second before he darts toward you, tugs your arm, and says, "Hurry. We're playing Labor or Porn." Jill is left behind.

"What are the rules?"

Cold Sore points at the projection screen and says, "You look at the woman's face and decide if she's on the verge of popping or having anal sex."

On the screen, you see the face of a screaming woman. She's giving Jamie Lee Curtis a run for her money. You want to climb into her mouth and hide behind her back molar, begging her to shut up, making it impossible to be found. If only there wasn't that gap between her front teeth.

Finally, someone shouts, "Labor!" It takes you a beat to realize that it was you shouting. A few women clap in agreement.

Another one says, "Can you fucking wait two seconds? I'm still contemplating."

Thank the woman for taking the game seriously.

Even though they're betting with Monopoly money, that doesn't make them any less fierce.

"Labor," the woman finally agrees.

It does turn out to be labor. Feel pretty goddamned good about yourself. "You would know," Marcia comes up behind you and whispers in your ear.

"Two months ago, Jill's baby bump disappeared," Marcia says. "There were a lot of rumors. No one knows what was true."

"What was the gossip?"

"Just be kind," she says. "Imagine what it's like to lose a child."

Suddenly, you wish you did a few lines of coke with Jill and Meth Head. You've never done coke, but there's a first time for everything. She's nowhere around. You sprint to the parking lot and she's about to drive off. She rolls down her window and you say, "Can I come with you?"

She gives you a half-smile and says, "You heard."

"Sort of. Not everything," you say.

She looks down. "Don't pity me," she says.

"Come back in," you say.

"I can't," she says. "A baby shower isn't about the baby. It's a funeral. It's about saying goodbye to the woman who's going to be a mother. She's moving on and she will leave you behind and this is your last chance to say, 'I will miss who you once were.'"

"For me. Please," you plead.

She gets out of the car. Across the parking lot, you see a body. It appears to be glowing. It takes a second to realize the glowing is Jackie's body. You've heard that women glow when they're pregnant, but this is more than skin radiating. So much more. It's almost supernatural in its charge. You want to yell, "It's about time you made it," but you can't. Her glowing is so bright you can't do anything except take it all in.

Jill is squinting. As if the sight in front of her is an eclipse. And she made the mistake of looking. And so did you. But you can't turn away. The glare begins to hurt your eyes. Your pupils burn. Like God has decided to make you see more than you can bear. Are you going to go blind? Jackie is coming closer and closer, and with each step she takes toward you, the less of her you can see.

On Apology

Twenty years after the gay bashing, I wrote an essay about the incident. Over the years, my friends became bored with me talking about the attack. They told me to publish the piece and then move on. I did what they said. I still couldn't let go. The images haunted me: I watched men attack my friend for being gay in the middle of the road. From a short distance, I saw everything happen and I did not intervene. I ran. I left my friend for dead.

Like most essayists, I was not interested in simply describing the particular incident. A gay bashing is a gay bashing. As a gay man, I have a heightened awareness that gay men are beaten all the time. I knew better than to think that there was something unique in this event. I wanted to employ the tragedy as a vehicle for making a larger, less obvious comment about human nature. In a way, you could say I was uninterested in myself, which may be hard to believe, even for me to believe.

Another way to think about it: I wanted the "I" to drop out of the essay and become about the world we live in. Maybe if I took another twenty years to write the piece, after this particularly tragic moment of history when hate crimes against gay men, and all minorities, have reached an apex, I would have had the makings for a great personal essay. In the present political climate, everything becomes a testament to suffering, which might be a good thing even if it is limited and exactly the sort of victim narrative you don't want to create.

It needs to be stated that a year after the gay bashing, my friend and I stopped talking. There was nothing more to say: He was beaten. I fled. It was a neat, clean story that found its end.

Although everything I'm writing is true, you should not overlook the element of dishonesty. My primary reason for writing the essay was that I missed my friend, even after approximately twenty years, and I wanted to reestablish contact. I didn't feel I could simply write an email that would seem spontaneous and say, "Hello." I needed to have a reason. What better reason is there than to say, "Here is an essay I published about you. I thought you may want to read it"?

After the essay was published, I told my husband I was going to search for him, and he asked if I harbored romantic feelings toward him, and I said, no, and he believed me, and that was that. After I mitigated my husband's fears, I asked myself if I was, indeed, telling the truth. It took me a moment: I was telling the truth. Even though my life has been a pleasant disappointment, my husband (in most ways) did not contribute to its blatant failures and a few isolated successes.

Truth be told, even after twenty years, I did miss graduate school. I possessed more and better friends. When I moved to the small, rural village where I teach creative writing, I found that most of my colleagues had children and befriended colleagues who had children. I was adrift. Once or twice I was asked to babysit, but the children found me unengaged and I was never asked to help again. The children were correct in their assessment. I was uninterested in them. I simply wanted them to like me so their parents would want to have me around. I find children invariably boring and useless.

I expected to find out that my friend had children. He came from a huge Mormon family and always dreamed of finding a boyfriend from India (for various reasons, he fetishized the culture in an annoying way) and raise children. These seemed like attainable desires and people's fantasies of themselves often come true. I imagined that his kids were nice and raised well. They would not allow an innocent man to be beaten in the middle of the road.

After the gay bashing, I never apologized to my friend for abandoning him. At the time, I felt that if I did say I was sorry, I would have to accept that I did something reprehensible, which was too much to handle. I needed to see myself as a victim, which I was. The men wanted to kill a faggot. Fortunately, I was not the one they caught.

You could say that my essay was anything but an apology. I acknowledged that I had done something wrong, but the self-reflection also functioned as a way of letting myself off the hook. It essentially said, "Through the essay I wrote, I self-reflected. Now I am allowing myself to be free." Perhaps it would be more appropriate to say the essay was a perfectly crafted apology: I didn't need anyone to accept its request, because I had already forgiven myself.

I stalled in searching the Web for him out of fear that he achieved a number of successes I predicted: a huge salary (I made $50,000); a perfect house (we still rent); a blessed interior life (my depressive episodes can worsen). However, even with those differences, I felt that my published essay would eclipse his successes in one way: I made something. Out of us.

Everything I had predicted turned out to be true: He was vice president of sustainability measures at a huge corporation; he possessed the most stylish apartment; he had kids; he was doing good in the world—surely, he saw life as urgent and good.

There was only one thing I was not jealous of.

He had been murdered.

*

He kissed me once. I'm not sure why he did it. It was not a spontaneous, romantic kiss. It was not a kiss that would have led to sex, even bad, pointless sex. After the kiss, we never talked about it, partly because there was nothing to say: It seemed less consequential than if our arms had touched on an armrest in a movie theatre, or if I had not known he was in the bathroom and opened the door. It was a kiss without consequence or meaning, which feels, in retrospect, like some sort of accomplishment, if only a name could be attached to such an act. At the same time, now when I shut my eyes and imagine the kiss, I envision that I am kissing the lips of a corpse, one that has been dead for a long time. From the newspaper articles, I cannot tell how long it took for someone to find him dead in his apartment. Because he was demonstrably rich, I assume it took a long time to find him: No one intrudes on a wealthy man's privacy. But it could have also taken a short time: He was powerful and people depended on him for guidance and support. I wonder if the escort/murderer kissed him on the lips before he stabbed him to death. It would help me to understand more fully my kiss with him if I could compare it with someone else he kissed. Because the newspaper saw the situation as one fueled with drugs and alcohol, I wonder if they even took the time to kiss. From talking to addicts, meth excites you to have sex immediately, not engage in foreplay. On the other hand, marijuana makes you want to kiss slowly. I wonder if he had been smoking pot before he knocked on my door and kissed me. I know he was not doing meth. I hadn't even heard of meth when we were in graduate school together. Sometimes when I remember us kissing, I imagine him leaving. For me, if there was, and there certainly isn't, any significance to the kiss, it's the fact that I shut my eyes during and after and did not move until I heard the door shut behind him.

Once I had a boyfriend, who is still alive although I have lost contact with him, too. Our time together was always spent in his apartment. Unlike myself, he owned a bed. When we woke up in the morning, I always made breakfast. This was not a result of me feeling the need to show appreciation for whatever we did or did not do. I served the meal so that he would have no reason to leave the bed. His comfort was irrelevant to me. When I left, which I always did after I made his meal, I liked my final image of him to be as minimal as possible: a man in bed, watching me leave. I wanted to suspend him in Time so that my life felt more contained, dispassionate, logical.

I ask my husband if he would want to make love to my corpse. He is a patient man and deals with my questions in a humane way. He smiles (faintly) and then moves on to a description of a TV show he wants us to watch together. When I pressure him to answer, he excuses himself to go to the bathroom. His behavior is one of the reasons our relationship has sustained itself over two decades.

Sometimes I need to know the truth and this is where our problems can begin. They are not major problems. If they were, I don't think our relationship would be a good experience for either of us. At the same time, you never know. "Would you make love to my corpse?" I ask.

"Would it smell?" he says.

This is one of the ways in which he has failed me as a husband: He responds to my probing, sincere questions with comedy.

"Of course," I said.

"Then no."

If I had known my friend was dead, I would never have written the essay about the gay bashing, which feels like a significant confirmation of an intimate truth, but I'm not sure why or what that truth (or truths) is/are.

As I grow older, I am consumed with elegies. Perhaps that's not exactly true: I've always been obsessed with the dead. As I am a teacher of creative nonfiction, I am always looking through literary magazines for an essay that deals with the loss of someone significant or even insignificant. A lot of these essays are mawkish in a (possibly) inoffensive way. They are saying, "I knew him and this is why he is special." I do not know why my friend was special to anyone except for the reasons that made me avoid him (wealth, unbridled happiness, children, etc.). Perhaps essays have nothing to do with apology or the dead. Perhaps an essay is akin to a kiss, something that could lead to heartbreak, or something that could be aborted and its origin replaced with words, simple and hermetic.

A Letter to David Buckel

LGBT civil rights lawyer and environmental activist David Buckel engaged in self-immolation to protest fossil fuels for their destruction of global welfare.

I dream of sounds: a body burning in the middle of Brooklyn Park, gasoline dousing the body of a man, the light, the flame, the drop of a plastic ziplock bag on grass. Yes, in my dreams, I can hear that tiny of a sound.

I don't know if I should hear those things. I doubt that I have the right to write about you. At the same time, you wanted witnesses. I was not there. Can you be a witness even if you're not present?

You are the kind of gay man that I aspired to be, but was too lazy to ever become. You wore nice-fitting suits, sported a nice buzzed haircut, and always looked like you had an idea spinning in your brain. There's something about a man who knows his next thought could be his best. It gives you good posture. Smart ideas refuse to slouch.

At least that's what it looks like in the photos I've seen. As you know, we've never met. I didn't even hear of your name until the newspaper headlines announced your death. I've found that most people, even my gay friends, have never heard of you either.

I apologize.

That's why I'm writing this letter. I'm telling you I see you even though you're gone. Of course, there's other reasons that I won't realize until I've finished this essay. You never truly understand what you said until after you've said it.

More dreams: you spinning around the courtroom. Me, on a jury. I'm always hoping you land in front of me. Desire of any sort makes me dizzy. It always has. At the end of the proceedings, the jury and I go into the back room and debate your claims. We talk about you like a father that we cannot disappoint. You're a moral man. Morality likes to believe it will always win. You can hear it clear its throat when a jury makes the wrong decision.

You fought for justice. You fought for murdered queers, raped trans men and women, suicidal gay elders, homosexuals wanting to secure their love. Their cases turned out to be some of your victories. For the ones who died, who never saw your grace, I hear them. They salute you. I want to touch faces of the dead. Their bodies bang against a wall like a gavel.

This essay is not an elegy. Is it wrong to try to create a body with words? To me, you are all ideas and hidden light.

I can't bring myself to say the clumsy word: self-immolation. Before you, I thought only of Buddhist monks in their gowns, speedy army officers, lonely student heroes, brave women, and sad nuns. History offers you a future, an affirmation, a path.

I disagree with those who said you had a death wish. You chose life. You choose life for us all.

I imagine myself as the yellow police tape stretched around your burning, encompassing as much as I can of your spirit. I imagine myself as the anguished trees, their branches still glowing from the heat, scared they, too, could be lit on fire. I imagine myself as a park bench, bitter someone may take me up on my offer and ask if I could offer them a place to rest. I imagine myself as bitter, burdened grass. I imagine myself as wind, taking what is not mine, and spreading it to those who don't know of their need. I imagine myself as the filthy stars, the ash-ridden, nasty half-moon.

I make you a promise: I will never imagine myself as you.

For the past few months, I have had even more dreams. The ziplock bag contained a note from you. Among other things it said: "Sorry about the mess." I dream of myself as a member of the sanitation crew assigned to the remains of your charred body. What does one wear for such a job? Should not one dress up for such an occasion? What do you do with the ashes?

I ask such stupid questions.

I dream of stealing the plastic bag with your remains.

How would I say to my beloved husband, *I encountered Death today. I wiped it off my hands. I washed it all away.* I think of my husband watching me hunched over the bathroom sink, scrubbing and scrubbing, looking at me only to say: *You'll never be clean. You never were.* Cleanliness has chapped my hands.

An essay is by its nature unclean. My husband asks if I should write this. It has nothing to do with you. He doesn't want me to be sad.

*

Let me tell you why he's scared of a burning. Your burning. He knows I wanted to die.

Not as a political statement. But out of sadness, chemical despair.

In school, I was hit and slapped and kicked. Like so many gay men are. You know our story. To some, we are dirty. To others, we are clean. God never washes His hands of us. Sometimes we wish He did. Before my high school graduation, I said to my teacher: *They will mock me when you say my name.* He said, *We'll be presenting you with an award.* I said, *They will boo me.* He said: *Then they will.*

They didn't. They gave me applause. I can still hear it.

Graduate school gave me a husband. During one argument, he said, *You are crazy and insincere.* That's the first time I knew he loved me.

Someone understands me, I thought.

I found a teaching job. He moved with me. That is all love does: It takes you from one place to another. You don't even know it until you've arrived. I liked my job. I thanked God for the labor, His love, my husband. I swore I would never defy my friends, colleagues. Labor is more than time and money. It is a way of claiming space in the world. I thought no one would ever want to take that space from me.

School is not the real world, they say. This is not true. It works the same way: There is an argument between two people. And then worse: an accusation. Accusations do not lead to conversation. They lead to more accusations. My labor turned out to be in peril.

I became ill. I didn't know the name of the sickness. No one did. But I could feel the pain. Once I went into my school office and plotted my death. I asked for help. God arrived instead. And then the doctors. Doctor after doctor. More pain. They hid me in a room with no doors, no windows. Doctors came and went. One said, *You're a writer. Write your story. Here are some pills. Go.*

My husband reminds me you died for a story *you* wanted to tell. The story of the earth. You died for the trees, the sky, the birds, the water, the clouds.

I lived in libraries, the empty aisles, the bathrooms. Once when I was young, I went there to be touched. Knowledge has never been enough. I needed to feel. Pick up enough books and you forget about trees, skies, birds, rivers. Hush. You can hear the waterfall. You can hear the morning bird songs. Hush. You can hear God slashing the sky to see us.

I am a petty person. I think dumb things. I think of your suicide note.

I picture you using a fountain pen, the kind one uses for special invitations, as yours was. I can hear the pauses between the curves and the lines. Each dot and curl matters. God kisses them.

And then there's the folding of the paper. We press. God presses. God kisses the creases. What falls inside the creases is prayer. What falls inside is the smoke. Look, David. Look, Lord. Touch the flames. Caress them. Breathe them in. Allow your lungs to blacken and rot.

David, I shut my eyes and allow the fire to singe my breath. I am nothing like a fire. I am not one who will burn. But I thank the Lord for you, my dear, dead David.

Two Truths and a Lie

I was still drunk from the night before. I asked a student to read their writing exercise. It was a fiction writing class. Their assignment was to create three different stories—one auto-biographical, the other fictions. The game was called Two Truths and a Lie. I stole the idea. I couldn't remember where. I drank a lot back then. I forgot a lot of things. Including my own stories. Like the name of the stale cologne the guy was wearing the night before. (Can cologne ever be stale? Can it go bad? Are there expiration dates on the bottle?)

The student was not cute. I didn't want to sleep with him/ never would sleep with him. Unless he was at my favorite dance bar Cosmos and there was no one left to take home and no one had turned on the lights. I didn't mind throwing myself on someone as long as I could deceive myself into thinking they were attractive.

"Can I begin?" he said. I couldn't tell if he was being rude or professional. Whatever it was it pissed me off. At the time, I didn't realize professionalism was by its nature rude. Part of me wanted to tell them that I was drunk, why I was drunk, and that I would continue to drink until I got bored with my misery, which I would, as I always did.

"By all means," I said, which made me laugh, not entirely because I was drunk, but now I sounded so professional. *By all means.* I've never used that phrase since. Perhaps I knew I was inviting something into the classroom, my life, and I just didn't know it yet. I was saying, *World, come on in and show me what you've got.* Perhaps that's why I was drinking so much: I secretly knew the world had a lot to show me. I was young enough to trick myself into thinking I knew it all. That's the difference between the young and the old: The latter knows there are still surprises in life.

"Here's story number one," he said and then cleared his throat. Young professional orator he was. "My father was shot in a 7-11."

I bit my tongue. I had to be careful. This wasn't a good time to be drunk. You could say the wrong thing and your career would be over. The class was a bit shocked. I think they all wrote that one off: a lie. No one would be that direct. Unless you were drunk and he certainly was not that.

"Anything you want to add?" I said tentatively.

"Less is more," he said. It took me a beat to remember that wasn't my wisdom. But a cliché. That's how out of it I was.

"OK," I said. "Story number two."

"I'm adopted. When my mother gave birth to me, there was a problem and she died. But I made it. Ta-dah!"

I'd never heard a quieter class. I excused myself to go to the bathroom. I grabbed my backpack which I had tossed on the desk and didn't remember bringing. I thought maybe I had brought some food. But there wasn't anything except a few Cheetos at the bottom, which I ate. There was only one other thing: a small bottle of cologne. I opened it and took a swig and then another. I needed to get my mind back in the game. But then I thought, am I stupid? Why wake myself up? Do I want this class to become a memory? But then I stopped thinking. I had to get back and teach, whatever that meant.

"I have one more," he said. It pissed me off. I knew there was one more. I didn't need to be told that.

"Story number three. My brother hurt himself in a quarry and is now a paraplegic," he said.

There was dead silence. "So," he said in the sweetest voice. "Which one is the lie? Which is the lie?"

No one knew what to say. I didn't know what to say. I was lost. I did what anyone else would have done. There was no choice in the matter. It had to be that way. I turned my back to the class, took out the cologne, and did a shot. And then another. And then whipped back around and thought about how gross the cologne was, I was, the student, his stories, the class, the game, the fiction writing, the truth telling, the world. And once I could barely take it, my fuzzy mind taken to the brink, I threw up. It wasn't a lot. It was like somewhat thick streams of dribble. But it was enough for a memory. Now they had to choose, they had no choice, it had nothing to do with me, it had to do with them, and the fact that they had to decide between truth and lies. Which I created in front of the class, I wasn't sure. But there was a choice to be made.

"I see flies, I see mosquitos, but I have never seen a gay man."

—A Chechen's woman response to the torture,
arrest, and murder of gay men in her country
as reported by the *New York Times*

I see trilobites. I see albino squirrels. I see the glasswing butterflies, I see sea salp, I see deep sea worms, I see sea sapphires. I see Cranchiidae, too. I see ectoparasites. I see the tick that infected my friend with psychiatric Lyme's disease. She stopped working due to exhaustion. She didn't qualify for disability so she opened up an Airbnb. I see centaurs. I never saw Pegasus. I do not see sirens or dragons or leviathans. I have never seen a UFO. A woman down the block did. She said it looked like a neon Rubik's cube. I hated those stupid puzzles. I did see ways I could cheat my mother whenever I played Uno. I could see the tell in my father's face when he played poker with friends. I don't see winners. Or losers. I see rickety voting machines. I see the objective to chess and Monopoly and bikinis and Chippendale dancers and adultery. I see the extra day for leap year. I see my fortune teller's message to me: "Hold tight." But I don't get what it means. I did not see the $43 my cousin took from me to buy cigarettes on the Native American reservation. I see the secondhand smoke, I see myself breathing it in (happily).

I see myself as a fat, middle-aged gay man who has never left the United States. Except once. I saw Beijing and saw the Great Wall of China. (It was sort of boring.) I see a pair of young gay men in my composition class holding hands. I see myself angry, I see myself feeling taunted, I don't see my husband and I ever kissing each other in public. I see my own gum disease, I don't see any children in my future, I see people asking us why, I see my husband shrugging his shoulders. I see myself a decade ago, sick and desperate, visiting all kinds of specialists. I see myself as a college instructor, privileged to have time to see all those doctors who saw nothing wrong with me except for the way I saw myself. I see London, I see France, I see my husband in his Lucky Charms pajama pants! I don't see America. Where are you? I see Russia.

O Russia! My neighbor lived through the Holocaust. She never wore short sleeves. But once in fifth grade I saw the tattooed number on her arm. (I can still see it.) "I see! I see! I see!" I boomed. I thought it was cool. I wanted one just like hers. I found a marker and wrote some random stuff on my arm. I showed her. My mother grabbed me and shook me. And then shook me some more. It was the first time I saw what hate felt like. I see rainbow necklaces! I see old-age bitterness as sexy. I do not see lava lamps or hula hoops or mood rings or pet rocks or Cabbage Patch kids or Pez dispensers.

Why can't I see America? Do I need a magnifying glass? I see my mother struggling to pay the rent after working two jobs. Now I see my student—a mother with three kids—living in the Econo Lodge after losing her federal financial aid due to a bad GPA. I see myself giving her an undeserved A. I see my boss calling me in and saying, "We're not doing welfare here." I see myself confused. I see leaks. From dams and my childhood aquarium. I don't see them coming from the White House. I refuse to see the broken bones and bruises of Russian gays. I will not see their body cut up by barbed-wire fence. I will not see them clubbed to death. I will not see soldiers making them lie on the ground so they can step and snap their necks with their boots. I cannot see those images. I see a Chechen woman standing in a field alone, teeth chattering, wondering where her vision will take her.

Are You There Judy?
It's Me, Steve.

I can still remember the fun in being a closeted gay junior high kid reading aloud the dirty parts of Judy Blume's *Forever* with a bunch of unpopular, smart girls. We hid from our teachers and fellow students during recess, hiding behind bushes, giggling over the passages describing sex between Katherine and Michael, the explicit details of their bodies rubbing against one another, leading to more explicit sexual behavior. Sometimes we skipped over the scenes of actual sex and moved on to one of our favorite parts: the scene in which Michael reveals his penis's nickname, Ralph.

We never knew why he chose that name.

The girls asked me if my penis had a name. It was one of the few times when I was around them that I remembered I was a boy. When I read passages from *Forever* in front of an audience of girls, I became Katherine, that female narrator, and I was so happy to be someone else. She was full of so much strength, frustration, and fear that I identified with her more than any male protagonist. My queer identity disappeared, an identity that I didn't have the courage to embrace wholeheartedly, and I could latch onto those heroines, merge my personality with theirs, pretend that their narratives were my own.

I never felt much attraction to the popular books that dealt with male rites of passage. They always seemed oddly dull. I tried to read *Lord of the Flies*. It was about a bunch of boys stranded on a deserted island who have to fight for their survival. Not only did they war with nature, but also among themselves. I felt a faint identification with Piggy: bumbling and a bit desperate, physically graceless, clinging to my Coke-bottle-thick glasses. I couldn't believe he persevered for as long as he did after his glasses were smashed. If mine broke, I knew that that would be the end of me. I never did finish the book. It was too painful to read the rest after Piggy's tragedy; I threw the book into the fireplace when no one was looking. I always suspected, probably unfairly, that Piggy was a closeted young homosexual: smart, cultured, unloved, cramming food in his mouth as a substitute for his failure to be touched, desired.

I, too, was well-read and gaining weight quick. So scared of my own queerness, I didn't want to have any proof of what could happen to me, even if that proof was a fiction. I knew that I deserved to triumph, and Blume's young female narrators revealed that potential.

One of the wonderful things about Blume's books was reading the way her descriptions of sex oscillated between the emotional and the clinical. A lot of her scenes involved lengthy conversations about desire, both the male and female openly admitting their excitement and reservations about taking the next step. As a closeted gay kid, I fantasized about meeting someone as cool as Michael, as articulate and as resourceful as Katherine. In one chapter, after her grandmother sends her birth control information, Katherine makes an appointment at the Planned Parenthood clinic. She receives a pelvic exam and a prescription for birth control pills. Blume presents the narrative in a matter-of-fact way, which makes the reader that much more comfortable if she chooses to emulate Katherine's actions. There's nothing odd or inherently dramatic in taking care of one's body. As a closeted gay kid, I didn't know what precautions I should take with mine. What health concerns were different for a gay man than a woman? No book answered that, at least none that I was aware of.

Of course, critics freaked out and criticized the book. Lou Willet Stanek in *The Arizona English Bulletin* referred to *Forever* as a "problem novel . . . that is as explicit as a sex manual." But through seeing Katherine deal with her needs so deftly, even insisting that Michael use a condom during sex, I imagined that one day I could engage in healthy sex, maturely and with the necessary protections. People were out there offering the information, and all you had to do was ask.

For me, the scariest parts of *Forever* involve the character of Artie. Artie is the boyfriend of Erica, who is Katherine's best friend. Blume constructs many extended scenes between Artie and Erica discussing sex, emphasizing Artie's fear, a fear so significant that he does eventually confess his ultimate terror: His impotence may be connected to his suspicion of his own homosexuality. This was not the sort of gay character I wanted to represent me. If any of the girls on the playground began talking about Erica and Artie, I deflected the conversation back to the fun sex scenes, praising Katherine for wanting to play dirty-word Scrabble. How I marveled that she possessed enough confidence to think of enough words for the duration of an entire match! I loved her; I wanted to be her.

But Artie creeped me out. I wanted him to disappear from the book, and sure enough, he does. After Erica breaks up with him, we find out that Artie tries to hang himself:

"On Thursday morning, Michael's birthday, Artie hung himself from the shower curtain rod in his bathroom. Luckily, the rod broke and he fell into the tub, winding up with a concussion and an assortment of cuts and bruises." It's never said why Artie tried to kill himself, but we can infer based on his earlier pronouncement. Michael admits to not having listened to him (was he afraid that he might be implicated if his friend came out? was he scared of his own urges?); Erica confesses her own heartlessness in breaking up with him so abruptly. In a novel obsessed with allowing the characters to talk at such seemingly unedited length, it comes off as a surprise that we never are given a scene that allows Artie to explicitly name the reasons behind his suicide attempt. In fact, he never enters the novel again, and I remember being happy that Blume kept him at a distance. His unabashed homosexual panic didn't lead anywhere constructive, and I needed possibility, not another representation of a suicidal closeted gay teen who seemed to be a failure on every level, even his inability to orchestrate a successful suicide.

If someone was going to be a victim, I wanted them to be at least a full-bodied, three-dimensional character. That was what I got from the next book of hers I read: *Blubber*. But having reread *Blubber* recently, essentially the story of the trials and tribulations of a fat girl, I was surprised by how much the book avoids the pitfalls of a traditional victim narrative. The story focuses on the relationship between three girls: Linda, the geeky, fat girl; Wendy, a pretty, obnoxious teen, who wants to humiliate Linda; and Jill, a friend of Wendy's, who slowly comes to empathize with Linda, and eventually tries to rescue her.

I remember reading the first scene of the book in which the fat girl Linda Fischer gives a report on whales. Linda's obliviousness of course allows Wendy, her main nemesis, a perfect opportunity to humiliate her in front of an entire class. What is remarkable about this setup is that Linda in a way is complicit in her own humiliation. Her debasement becomes predicated on her inability to foresee the dangers in giving a speech about an animal (the whale) she resembles. You can't help but read the scene and feel frustration toward Linda for not avoiding the inevitable through self-awareness.

Scenes like this affected me in a profound way. As a visibly gay kid growing up, I wondered how much of my pain was self-inflicted, how much was beyond my control? By identifying with this narrator, there were no easy answers, no matter how much I wanted them out of sheer convenience, the understandable desire for scapegoating. Gym class was always the predictable place for emotional torture. I remember having to do laps around the gymnasium. A group of kids would always follow me and punch me in the arm, try to trip me. Sometimes I would deliberately fall to the ground, make a spectacle of my plunge, just so they would receive their entertainment and then go away, harm someone else.

My best friend Alicia was as large as Linda, but no one teased her. She would turn out to be my closest queer alliance, and bodyguard. If anyone would give me a hard time, she would frighten them off, stare them down, raise her fists. Not only was she tough, she was smart. No way would she ever be seen as doing something as idiotic as giving a speech about the humpback whale to a bunch of bored teens.

When *Blubber* was released, I remember reading reviews in the school library. I recently managed to find one of them in a critical study of Judy Blume; of *Blubber,* the critic Richard Jackson said, "I think Judy is saying something quite nervy in this book: that is, there are some people who, because of the way they behave, inspire cruelty. I think one of Judy's points is you can cast yourself into a loser role. And that's your choice."

When I first had read this interpretation as a preteen, I felt exhilarated and frightened. Was my ridicule a result of my inability to disguise my queerness in a more successful manner? In gym class, I did run away from the soccer ball whenever it darted in my direction. It was my choice to always tag along with the girls during recess, avoiding my male classmates who liked to climb the jungle gym, play Smear the Queer on the blacktop. I could change. All I had to do was put my mind to it.

Unable to claim ignorance, I knew why people singled me out for ridicule; my self-insight should be able to help me alter my social situation.

But at the same time, there was only so much I could change about myself. If Linda lost weight, other people's respect for her would increase. Specific markings of my queer identity—my whiny voice, effeminate nature—could only be changed so much. I was who I was. Walking bowlegged and talking in a deep voice could only conceal my essential nature for so long, and how convincing would such changes be?

Growing up, I often spent a lot of time with my uncle. Even though no one would openly say it, everyone knew he was gay, and no one cared. He was a sweet guy, and when he came over, he told me stories about a man named Oscar Wilde. He never once said that Wilde was gay, but explained that a lot of "people in power were jealous that he had really intense relationships with young people."

"Why did people care?" I asked him.

"People don't like people who have a lot of friends," he said. "They get jealous."

He then told me that the "people in power" tried to hurt Wilde, because they were so intimidated by his social skills. They put him on trial and tried to condemn him. I loved the idea of a trial, and the fact that someone, according to my uncle, could be sentenced to death for simply being friendly fascinated me.

I liked myself for being such a social outcast, someone no one paid attention to. No one wanted to be my friend, especially young people. I was safe from the cruel world.

One time I told him about *Blubber* and read aloud to him the climatic scene, which involves a trial. I thought for sure he'd appreciate it, and his approval of me mattered. In the scene, Linda is put on trial by her classmates, led by Wendy. Only one student attempts to protect Linda, a girl named Jill, who has always been disturbed by Linda's victimization. Jill demands that Linda receives a lawyer, someone to defend her. Infuriated, Wendy turns on Jill, mocking her. By defending Linda, Jill suffers from serious social fallout, being the last one chosen for a sports team and ending up having no partner for a school trip.

As I was reading the scene about Jill, my uncle stopped me mid-sentence and exclaimed, "That's why no one defended Oscar Wilde."

I didn't understand the connection.

"Everyone was afraid that they would be identified with him."

I was still confused, so I let him try again to make necessary correlations.

"Victimization is contagious. Or so people think. If you hang around a victim, you'll become one yourself."

"Jill doesn't end up a victim," I said. "If you let me finish, you would have found out that she fights back against Wendy."

"Good for her," my uncle said. "You should follow her example."

He paused and then said, "There have been so many times in my life I wanted to be like Jill. But I've always kept my mouth shut."

"Everyone likes you," I said.

"They like what I allow them to know about me," he said.

I got nervous, so I said, "Let me finish the scene."

My family members always became skittish about my obsession with Judy Blume. When my mother discovered that I was reading *Are You There God? It's Me, Margaret,* she forbid me to read it, grabbing the book from my hands and then hiding the book in her bedroom.

"That book divulges women's secrets," she said.

"The fact that a woman gets a period is a national secret?" I said.

"Don't be a smart mouth," she said. "It's just something you shouldn't read. It's a book for women by a woman. Men have no right in reading in it. Even sweet little boys like you."

"But I'm curious."

"Be curious about your own sexuality. Leave ours alone."

What I failed to tell my mother was that I couldn't be curious about my own sexuality; I feared that if I found out something in a book, I would turn out to be one of them—a doomed, suicidal, teen homosexual who would be used by abusive, older men. I was convinced I was the only boy in the world grappling with his sexuality.

My favorite scenes in *Are You There God? It's Me, Margaret* revolved around Margaret and her new friends' secret club. I remember fantasizing about the fun they must have had in agreeing upon a name for their organization: the PTS club, or Pre-Teen Sensations. I loved the rules they had: They could not wear socks with their loafers, they each kept a Boy Book with a current list of the cutest boys. Another rule was they all had to wear bras no matter how flat-chested they were. And most importantly: "The first one to get her period had to tell the others about it. Especially how it feels."

At one PTS meeting, the girls compare their breasts to the ones of models in a *Playboy* magazine that Margaret steals from her father's dresser drawer. They end the meeting with the ritual of repeating the mantra "We Must Increase Our Busts" fifty times and other assorted exercises to accelerate their womanhood.

Blume describes the scenes in such an effective way. You can feel the joy, tension, and competitiveness in these girls' solidarity. Blume's talent as a writer partly came from her creating for us the opportunity to gaze voyeuristically at our own secrets. Through her empathy for her protagonists, she allowed us to identify with them so that our secrets conflated with theirs, and we could exhibit them, boldly, proudly, and happily.

Of course, my secrets didn't reveal themselves until college, but reading about the PTS club helped mitigate my frustration for a number of years. Eventually, I thought, I'll find a club of like-minded people, and we'll form our own group and silly rules.

I can still remember the first coming out group I joined at the University of Illinois at Urbana–Champaign. Everyone was uptight, nervous, constantly looking over their shoulder to make sure that no one was spying on them. You could also feel everyone in the room hoping they didn't appear as gay and as insecure as the person who just spoke. I remember spacing out as someone told his uneventful coming out story. I felt jealousy toward Margaret and her friends teasing one another, glad to be in each other's company.

Issues of truth and secrecy take center stage in *Are You There God? It's Me, Margaret.* One of the most tense scenes in the book occurs when Margaret finds out her friend Nancy has lied about her period: "I didn't know what to say. I mean, what can you say when you just found out your friend's a liar!" I imagined the day my friends would find out I was gay. Would they be similarly unempathetic in their reaction? How could I lessen the intensity of their reactions? Each day I waited in disclosing my sexuality, the more justification they had for a more volatile response. They would call me worse things than a liar.

When Blume started to write books for adults, people like my mother, I felt betrayed. Blume was supposed to be on our side. She had no right to show any empathy for anyone else other than kids. No author other than Blume managed to represent our hidden desires, to make a spectacle of our secret interiority. So when I snuck a peek at the back cover of my mother's copy of *Wifey*, I was enraged as I read one of the blurbs that exclaimed: "You will enjoy this book . . . HIDE IT WHERE THE CHILDREN WON'T SEE IT!"

How could Blume? How could she switch sides? There's no way she could keep our secrets intact. When you write about two opposing factions, you always take sides; it's inevitable. Blume was no longer an ally. At the same time I was curious about my mother's secrets, which I assumed were contained in the narrative of *Wifey*. I scanned the book for any clues.

The book revolves around the escapades of a bored housewife named Sandy Pressman. Her husband Norman is well-meaning, but a bit of a dolt. Sandy tried to find self-satisfaction in a series of escapades. I can still remember the scene in which Sandy confessed her boredom to a friend named Lisbeth. Lisbeth gives her some advice: She tells Sandy that she and her husband sleep with other people on Thursday nights. The only stipulation is that they're both required to tell the other every single detail about the encounter.

As Lisbeth declares, "Everything must be out in the open . . . that's the only rule . . . no secrets . . . this class I took last semester in Contemporary Relationships was fabulous . . . how it showed us how secrets cause strains. This openness has caused such a boon in our marriage."

Coincidentally, when I was secretly reading these sections, my parents' marriage was falling apart. My father was rarely coming home, sometimes disappearing for a few days at a time without even a phone call alerting us as to his whereabouts. My mother walked around depressed, going to bed around 6 p.m., forgetting to make me dinner.

One day I decided to confront her: "You and Dad are so unhappy."

"Tell me something I don't know."

"Maybe you should follow Lisbeth's advice."

"Who is Lisbeth?"

"Don't play dumb," I said.

"I have no idea who Lisbeth is."

"Lisbeth from the porn you read! Lisbeth and her husband who sleep with everyone in their town so they don't have to touch each other!"

"You're going into my room and reading my books?"

"At least I'm learning something from them," I said. "You're so stupid you're going to make Dad leave us. Let him sleep with someone else other than you."

My mother slapped me across the face. "He is doing that," she said. "He knows I know. That's why he can't face me. Or you."

I walked away and decided I'd stick to my own books, maybe even read something as tame as *Tales of a Fourth Grade Nothing*.

Once I wrote Blume a fan letter.

This was all I got back:

Dear Young Fan,

Thank you so much for your support and affection. Every writer is so dependent on their readers, and I am no different. I am happy that I managed to capture stories that felt like they happened to you. We can learn a lot from other people's stories.

This is the truth: I crumpled up the letter. It hurt me. For the same reason it healed me. It could have been written for anyone.

On Beauty

My mother was the ugliest woman in the rehab clinic. She sat alone at a table for dinner, and no one came near her. Did they fear ugliness was contagious? I wanted to ask the other septuagenarians. But I didn't. I was afraid. I had enough body issues of my own.

I took a certain amount of comfort that my mother looked so ugly. It could be translated to mean that she was suffering. So much so, the pain was distorting her body, seconds at a time, right in front of me. This made me think that the other patients' families felt pity for us. Maybe more than for their own sick relative. Through her ugliness, I became a spectacle myself, one that deserved special attention. I like attention and words of kindness. It made the fear of my mother's death that much less painful.

At the same time, I feared that my mother's ugliness caused people to guess that I was doing something wrong. Maybe she was the victim of elder abuse. When I talked to people other than my brother, I emphasized that I lived far away, that I barely talked to her. Once I even started saying that I didn't know why her front teeth were missing and she had cradle cap. Something I had never heard of before until the nurse told me. I wondered how long that had been building up.

She was suffering from Alzheimer's disease and uterine cancer. Her body and mind were tired. Washing her hair (I'm sure) was exhausting. Who could blame her? My own teeth and gums are in horrible shape. I'm always afraid that the decay smells bad so I cover my mouth when I talk. I don't know if it works. But it makes me feel better. Point is, to make yourself presentable can take a lot of effort, especially if your mind and body are failing.

Her fashion didn't help. Her favorite sweatshirt had a logo of Tweety Bird on it. She loved that shirt. When she moved into the clinic from the hospital, somehow the shirt got lost. She panicked. She said, "Where's my Tweety Bird? Where's my Tweety Bird?" It was bad enough that she resembled a kid who couldn't clean herself as it was, let alone chirped like some yellow fat-headed bird. She cried a few times every day about the shirt—it was the one thing she consistently remembered, even more than my brother's or my visits.

It was strange: Sometimes I felt beautiful around her like I never had before. I walked with more unaffected grace; I spoke with a greater clarity. I smiled more. Her decrepitude was the incentive I needed to look better. Her impending death made me look stunning.

There was a gay nurse I started to talk to. We walked around the halls together. He was a lot older than me. He used to work with AIDS patients in the early '80s. Lesions, he told me, make you look bad no matter what you do. No amount of base could conceal death.

One day he turned to me and said, "Do you want some free lipstick?"

"I'm not a drag queen," I said.

"I know," he said. "And I wouldn't care if you were."

And then he added: "For your mother. It might be nice to put some on your mother. She might look a little better."

I wanted to slap him. How could he insinuate my mother was ugly?

But I took the lipstick. I woke my mother up out of a dead sleep. She was groggy. She said she wanted to go back to bed. I didn't care. She needed the lipstick. If she wore the lipstick, everything would be fine. I wanted her to see that she could be, indeed, beautiful. Or not ugly. Or not the ugliest. It all came down to the lipstick.

She brushed me away. And then she relented.

I put on the lipstick pretty well. Not too many blotches.

Her roommate spoke for the first time since I had been there. I forgot she was even there. "Good try," she said. And then gave me a mirror.

"Thank you," I said.

I showed my mother, who had no response. She was tired. She put her head back down. I forgot to take a snapshot of her so I could remember her beauty. How could I forget? There she was, rolled over on her side, snoring, the lipstick smeared all over the pillow and the side of her face.

Self-Portrait as a 1980s
Cineplex Movie Theatre
(An Abecedarian)

Amadeus (1984)

I never knew who I wanted to be: Amadeus or Salieri?

In the movie, Amadeus wins. We know his music will live forever. The final scene shows us a decrepit Salieri in a wheelchair, rolling around in a nursing home, bellowing, "Mediocrities, everywhere! I absolve you! I absolve you all!"

When I was fourteen and watched the Oscars, everything changed. F. Murray Abraham, who plays Salieri, won the award for Best Actor, beating out Tom Hulce, who portrays Amadeus. In movie history, the role of Salieri will never be forgotten. Amadeus lost. Hulce's performance will never be as esteemed. Abraham went on to receive great stage roles on Broadway and even now, after all these years, shows up in popular, edgy HBO thrillers like *Homeland*.

No one else could have been a greater embodiment of Amadeus than Hulce. I never heard much about him again. *Amadeus* mostly disappeared. Hulce has directed a few mediocre TV shows. He did come out of the closet. I know he inspired me to publicly tell people I was gay. Which was a pretty brave thing to do in the mid-to-late '80s. Maybe his openness limited his acting options. I want to believe it did. The idea of him disappearing from film just because saddens me.

Perhaps maturity is realizing that you can't tell any difference between your successes and failures, the losers from the winners.

The Blues Brothers (1980)

I always wanted to be Aretha Franklin. I can't count the number of times I watched her big musical number. She plays a waitress at a greasy-spoon restaurant. Her lughead of a boyfriend demands that she cook him a meal. After all, he says, he is "the man and she is the woman." She responds in the perfect way. She sings "Respect." With a trio of singers, she struts around the restaurant, pushing him back with the simple wave of her finger. She moves in a way that's unique to her; it's not overly forceful. There's a lag between her steps. She knows things are going her way; there's no reason to exhaust herself. Once a roommate walked in on me when I thought I was alone. I was imitating Aretha's steady, undisturbed gait. She said, "What are you doing? It looks like you're walking underwater."

C. H. U. D. (1984)

In high school, I considered my classmates to be Cannibalistic Human Underground Dwellers, the ones from the monster movie C. H. U. D. They, too, seemed to rise from the ground and latch on to my feet, tripping me, laughing when my head hit and dented the locker. The leader apologized after his horde disappeared. He leaned in and kissed me. My teeth knocked against his. He held the sides of my head and said, "I want to give you my tongue." I took it. I was willing to take a lot back then. Afterward, I went into the bathroom. I didn't wipe the drool from my face. Never has being devoured felt so good. My tooth was chipped. Two days later I went to the dentist.

Dirty Dancing (1987)

During high school, I was obsessed with speech team. I loved getting up in front of a room full of people and a judge and reciting an oratorical declamation. Words were my music.

I was having the time of my life. I wish I could say I wanted to be a dancer. I've always felt out of touch with my body.

Once I was in a final round at a speech tournament. I was competing in a stand-up comedy category. There was a competitor who was better than me. Before things began, he said, "I'm better than you. Good luck anyway."

I disappeared into the bathroom. When I came back out, I went up to him and told him his speech coach needed to talk to him. He asked why.

"Your mother died," I said.

He immediately started crying. "I knew it was going to happen. She has been ill. But I didn't expect it to happen now," he said.

He walked away and didn't make it in time to perform. My lie worked. I won. Nobody puts Baby in the corner.

The Elephant Man (1980)

Do we all feel like the Elephant Man until we find someone who loves us? And is that feeling more than universal but infinite? Or, to evoke the final scene in David Lynch's film, are we waiting to hear our planetary maternal force tell us "no one will ever die" in order to know that we are as safe as a wounded child in a lonely bed?

Unlike me, my husband is not a crier. I've seen him cry only a handful of times in the fifteen-plus years we've been together. That final scene in *The Elephant Man* always gets to him. Does he feel that he's never found the love he wanted, even in me? Is he waiting for something greater? Is he disappointed in his willingness to settle for someone doomed always to be curiously earthbound?

Friday the 13th (1980)

I loved watching beautiful people die.

· Gandhi (1982)

No one knew who I was supposed to be for Halloween. They badgered me over and over again, threatening to rip off my toga if I did not tell them.

I did not tell them.

I kept silent.

The next day no one brought it up. And even if someone had, I wouldn't have said anything. Silence was crucial for me to master if I was ever to become wise.

The next Halloween I dressed up as Maria Shriver. Everyone got it right away.

The Hitcher (1986)

If a serial killer in a movie kidnaps the hero's girlfriend and chains her hands to a bumper of one semitruck, her feet to a different truck, we expect she'll be saved. Nobody thinks that he'll fail, that in this one case she'll really, truly get pulled apart.

Nobody expects to snap.

In my late thirties, I went into psychosis for the first time. For months, I couldn't sleep, concentrate, sit still, etc. No doctor could figure out what was wrong. I convinced myself that a Christmas stocking held a key to my illness. I told my husband that all the doctors had to do was stare at the stocking long enough for a secret sign; everything would then be solved. My husband said I would be healed as long as I didn't talk about the stocking. When I was alone with a doctor, I'd take it out of my backpack and try to explain.

One neurologist said, "Why don't you leave the stocking with me? I'll run some blood tests on it."

"Do you think I'm crazy?" I said. "You can't run blood tests on a stocking."

One day I went to Arby's and ordered a sandwich with fries. I became paralyzed I'd find something in them: hairs, dead bugs, and yes, even possibly—though I knew the chances were next to none—a severed finger.

I'm Dancing as Fast as I Can (1982)

What queer kid doesn't like musicals? When I opened the newspaper and saw the title *I'm Dancing as Fast as I Can*, I knew it was a must-see.

"I'm not going to take you to see that," my mother said. "It's not what you think it is."

"I must see it," I said. "Musicals make me happy. And we both know I'm not a happy kid."

"You're not going," she said. "I'm your mother. I know what's best for you. This is one of those times when you have to listen to me."

The movie theatre was located down the block. The film was starting in ten minutes. I insisted.

"Fine," she said. "I warned you." She was pissed. She kept her arms folded. She refused to look at me.

We made it just in time. You could tell she wished she had stalled. She did not want to see this movie. It was worse that it was with me.

My mother stared at me on and off for the entire running time. She was trying to read my facial expressions. She wanted to hear that I should have trusted her.

The movie is *not* a musical.

The film is about a successful documentarian named Barbara. She's a little high-strung. And then she becomes even more high-strung. She slowly grows addicted to sedatives. She decides to film a documentary about a woman who is dying of cancer. Barbara wants to give people hope. She doesn't want her movie to be relentlessly depressing. The cancer victim sees a rough cut of the film. She's enraged. She hates it. She tells Barbara that it's a lie. She tells Barbara she has no talent. Barbara's depressed. Her addiction to drugs begins to become overwhelming. She decides to stop cold turkey. She attacks her husband. He ties her to a chair. She ends up being institutionalized.

"So what did you think?" my mother asked. She put her hands on her hips.

I had no choice. I had to tell the truth. There was no other option except the truth.

I loved it.

Jaws (1980)

These days I may be a fat, middle-aged gay man. But when I was younger, I was lithe and quick, always eager to go swimming. My mother taught me. She says that she learned from growing up in an orphanage with many, many other children. They didn't have time to give all the kids lessons even though one of their primary outings was to go to a swimming pool. It was a cheap activity. The supervisors would demand that all the kids get into the pool; the ones who didn't would literally be thrown into it. "Sink or swim," they'd say. My mother swam. She taught me how to do the same. Swimming is fine when you want to do it. But sometimes the world outside your home can feel like it's just nincompoops pushing you into a pool, demanding that you panic over yet another fake shark. Swimming for your life can get exhausting. There are times when you feel tired and you want to go home.

The Karate Kid (1984)

Esther, my best friend in high school, found out that Ralph Macchio loved mandarin oranges. This fact was in *People* magazine. At one point, I could have told you the page number. Esther was obsessed with him. It was all we talked about.

I had never had a mandarin orange. I told this to Esther. "Not too many people like them. They're a delicacy. Like caviar," she said.

She became eerily invested in losing weight. She went on a new diet. She called it the mandarin orange diet. For a week, all she ate was mandarin oranges and protein shakes. It worked.

And then she stopped eating altogether.

Her parents took her to the hospital, where they force-fed her. She couldn't keep anything down. No one could solve the problem. Whenever she came back to school, she didn't stay long. She fainted a lot. During lunch, she'd always go to the bathroom. She smelled funny when she came back.

Once I took out a small can of mandarin oranges from my backpack. "Remember these?" I said.

She knocked them out of my hand. "I'm not stupid," she said. "You can't trick me to put food in my mouth."

She never talked to me again. She ended up being the first person I knew who died.

Little Shop of Horrors (1986)

If I could be reincarnated, I would want to come back as a Venus flytrap. The sheer spectacle of a talking plant with huge teeth killing dumb people was something not to be missed. I remember sitting feet away from the movie screen wanting to touch the plant's teeth, wondering how the special-effects men managed to create such a believable look.

I'm obsessed with teeth. For me, that's what I find to be most sexy: when someone has nice, clean, upstanding teeth. We grew up poor. When we became poorer, we stopped going to the dentist. For twenty years, I didn't have a checkup. I didn't do anything until I noticed that after every meal blood was in my mouth. The mashing of food irritated my gums no matter how slowly I went, how careful I was. Now my gums remain destroyed even after a half a dozen deep scalings, graftings.

The Muppets Take Manhattan (1984)

During our childhood, my brother and I bonded over movies. We lived in the middle of nowhere and rode our bikes to see *The Muppets Take Manhattan*. We both agreed that this was our favorite Muppet movie, because they were the star of the show; in the other films, they were often reduced to being mere props for the boring humans. When it came out on VHS, we watched the film at least fifty times, reciting the lines together. For us, it was *The Rocky Horror Picture Show*.

We assigned the roles ahead of time and always performed gracefully, never once stepping on the other's lines. Except for one. We both always wanted the role of Janice, the hippie saxophone player. My favorite scene is when the Muppets are all struggling to find an agent willing to take them on. Broke, they decide to crash at the bowling alley, catching some shut-eye in the lockers. Janice says: "I get the one with the Jacuzzi." My brother and I have never laughed harder in our lives. He became an accountant. He always goes to Las Vegas. He still hasn't moved out of his townhouse. I wonder how hard he plays at the casinos. Would he ever have enough for a Jacuzzi? If he owned one, would it give me the sense of security that he'll always be OK?

National Lampoon's Vacation (1983)

My family and I never went on vacation. Anywhere. Unless you count the local Putt-Putt golf course. I remember watching *National Lampoon's Vacation* and thinking it was the strangest satire; even with all the bad things that happen to them—a dog murdered by the family's failure to remember it was tied to the car bumper; being stranded in the desert; Christie Brinkley almost tempting Chevy Chase into adultery—it was hard for me to feel sorry for them. They were a family and they were on vacation. Their destination, Wally World, was obviously a play off Disney World, which was always my dream. Decades later, my husband took me there. His father always took his family. There was a sweet, elegiac feel to the trip. As we went through the endless lines to ride on the Tower of Terror and the Haunted Mansion, we laughed at all the tombstones etched with silly puns. His father loved cornball humor. "Here Lies Henry Blake, He Stepped on the Gas Instead of the Brake." I would usually be cynical, but it brought back so many good memories. I loved Disney's sentimentality and spectacle—two things which make America America. I never felt so proud to be an American as when I was there, saluting Mickey Mouse, watching the fireworks, admiring all the nuclear families that would disintegrate over time.

On Golden Pond (1981)

I fear my husband's death all the time. I talk about it so regularly that my husband finds it creepy, joking that I might be looking forward to it. It's just the opposite. I can't bring myself to watch On Golden Pond. The domestic drama revolves around an aging couple (Henry Fonda and Katharine Hepburn) who live in their lake house every summer. Their daughter, played by Jane Fonda, visits. Unsurprisingly, family conflicts ensue, especially when it's revealed the father is suffering from Alzheimer's disease.

The idea of my husband slipping into senility is too much for me. I promise myself that, no matter what, I'd take care of him, even if it meant I'd have to prop him up in the blue recliner and watch him gaze out the window for hours on end. Sometimes when he watches TV, I watch him watching TV. I'm always relieved when I ask him a stupid question about a show and he can organize all the plotlines with such dexterity, even if he's tired, ready to go to bed with me. I figure if he loses his mind, we'll skip the dramas and move on to the half-hour sitcoms, and if he can't follow those we'll just watch the commercials, selling us something we once thought we needed.

Porky's (1982)

I didn't have sex in high school. And then AIDS hit. So I waited some more.

Quicksilver (1986)

My friend was an extra in *Quicksilver*, a film about a manipulative stockbroker, who through one dumb move, loses everything and decides to become a professional bike messenger for a speed delivery firm. I'm still jealous that my friend got to see Kevin Bacon whizzing around streets among crowds of onlookers.

Screw the people who boasted they were a mere six degrees of separation from Kevin Bacon. I was two.

A definition of desire: seeing Kevin Bacon race past you for a film he knows will flop. He'll have no choice but to look back over his shoulder and make sure you're still there.

Romancing the Stone (1984)

My mother owned thousands of used Harlequin romances. She put them in bookshelves which plastered our walls in almost every room. It never occurred to my mother to write one herself. My father mocked her, demanding that she tell him why she needed to own more than one. They were the same old story, no?

In *Romancing the Stone*, Kathleen Turner plays a romance novelist who finds her life becoming intertwined with gun-toting henchmen, an exotic bird smuggler, and gaudy jewelry. About ten minutes before the end of the movie, my mother turned to me and said, "We need to leave."

"But they haven't kissed yet," I said.

"We need to leave," she said.

She told me she never liked to see the final minutes of a romantic movie. She confessed that she never reads the final pages of her romances. That's why she can read them over and over again.

I like to believe that if you don't make it to the end, there's always something one can mistake for possibility.

She's Having a Baby (1988)

Good for her.

The Terminator (1984)

How maudlin is it that whenever I hear Arnold Schwarzenegger's German accent, I imagine my biological mother who I will never meet? How shameful is it to admit that the plot of *The Terminator* matters more than any of its stunning action sequences? How embarrassing is it to confess that I wept during the tacked-on epilogue of a woman making a tape-recorded message for her son who she will never encounter?

At the heart of *The Terminator* is the story of a mother and a son doomed to never know one another. We all know the simple premise: A mother gives birth to a son who will become a hero in the fight to kill the machines that are taking over the human world. It is possible to shuttle through space and time to alter a small detail in human history that will change everything forever. That's why the mother must abandon her son: He won't feel the obligation to take care of her. He will go on his solo journey and become a leader. Mankind hangs in the balance.

I imagine what my mother would say in such a message to me. With my luck, I wouldn't be able to hear her words. Somehow they'd be garbled. Things get messed up when you're ricocheting through galaxies and eons. What if all I heard was the beat of silence that occurred as she went to press the stop button?

Even worse, what if I answered *that is more than enough* when all I wanted to hear was *I'll be back?*

Under the Cherry Moon (1986)

When my parents die, I will not receive an inheritance. Which doesn't bother me. I've never had any money and I never will. This fact never stopped me from dreaming of being Kristen Scott Thomas in *Under the Cherry Moon*. She plays a woman who inherits a $50 million trust fund on her twenty-first birthday.

There's only one catch: A gigolo named Christopher Tracy (played by Prince) and his partner in crime Tricky plan to seduce her and steal all her money.

Who wouldn't want to be swindled by Prince?

When the film began, my mother nudged me and asked me to tell someone that there was something wrong with the print. She didn't know it was filmed in black and white.

"Only old people watch movies that way," she said. "I'm paying for brightness. For hope."

Videodrome (1983)

You are a geeky president of a television company, determined to find a way of boosting falling ratings. You begin to receive access to some weird cable shows from a station in

Malaysia which no one seems to have heard of. The images are of anonymous people being raped and murdered. You find out that there's a plot by an evil conglomeration to fill the airwaves with shows that somehow have the ability to cause cancer in the viewing audience.

None of this feels real. It must be a nightmare. You wish you were sleeping. But you know you're awake when a slit appears in your stomach. The slit is so big you can fit a VHS cassette inside. So why not try? You grab a cassette and shove it into the slit. Somehow the images on the tape appear on the TV screen a few feet away from you.

For the first time in your life, you are on.

WarGames (1983)

I can still remember my first manic episode. It happened during graduate school when I was in Utah. This was the symptom: I couldn't stop walking. I had to be in motion. I ditched the classes I was supposed to teach. Standing in front of a classroom felt dangerous. Someone could get me.

I walked for miles. I called up my boyfriend and told him that I couldn't stop walking, that I didn't know what was happening, that I was so determined to keep moving I found myself failing to obey traffic lights. I didn't look both ways before I crossed the street.

When I could calm down, I called teachers and doctors and told them that I was terrified. Something was happening to my body.

I never slept. One day I woke up and everything felt strange. I called my boyfriend and he said, "Did you hear? Did you hear?" and I said, "Hear what?" And he said, "The Twin Towers collapsed."

Before he told me about the crashes, I always fantasized about being in the middle of a world war. It seemed like a cool thing. From time to time, I thought about the movie *WarGames* and how everything fell apart because of one entitled teenager. Matthew Broderick plays a kid who hacks into the wrong computer at the wrong time and almost accidentally starts a war with Russia.

In my paranoia, I couldn't help but think: Am I the one who brought this on?

I wasn't sure what this was.

All I know: Hours later, when I went to the hospital, I thought I was dying of a heart attack. Everything was crazy. The emergency room was in chaos. Everyone had something wrong with them. Everyone was suffering. The Twin Towers were ruining everything.

Except me. I suddenly felt much better. I'm not any more damaged than anyone else.

For the first time, life felt like the ending to *WarGames*. Everything was as simple as "the draw" in a tic-tac-toe game. There was only one mystery: For the first time in days, was I somehow ahead of the game?

Xanadu (1980)

An item on my bucket list: one complete whirl around a roller rink.

I've always wanted my life to become a dizzying blur of scantily clad men, neon lights, and Olivia Newton John's smile. Once every couple of years, I come close to that. And then it disappears. As quickly as the romantic musical *Xanadu* left the theatres.

But it doesn't matter to me. When Olivia Newton John and Michael Beck kiss for the first time, the movie bursts into an extended animated sequence. A tornado sweeps them away, somehow managing to shrink them to a size small enough to allow them to stand on top of a blooming rose.

They both jump and transform into bright fishes, happy to be teasing one another in the water, only to soon morph into birds flying high. One of them crash-lands into the sea only to be saved by the other. And finally, they both find their way back to the original rose, where they kiss and disappear.

I thought to myself: This is love. I still replay that scene in my mind, on my computer. I never tell my husband this. I want to keep it all to myself.

To be an academic is to always ward off the sentimental. *Xanadu* taught me otherwise. It taught me sometimes you need to be a bird or a fish or on top of a stupid rose.

Yentl (1983)

I've always been confused as to why Barbara Streisand's metamorphosis from young woman to young man was successful. I admire her character's decision to gender-switch in order to continue to study the Talmud after her father dies. She wants to learn even though strict Jewish religion doesn't allow women to participate.

But exactly how big a suspension of disbelief does one need to take in order to fall for her trickery?

I have no idea. In some scenes, the transformation looks convincing; from others, it's completely preposterous. I had the same reaction to Dolly Parton's breasts in *Rhinestone*. I could never quite tell if they were real. Once I confessed my confusion to my father. He said, "When it comes to tits, you just give in and believe."

I'm an obsessive person. At least four times I went to the theatre to watch *Yentl*. I tried to figure out under what lighting, what settings she looked best. I wrote all my observations in a notebook. I tallied the results. I wanted to find a pattern. I never did. It was and still remains a mystery.

Perhaps this is why I write personal essays, trying to find that pattern, catch the right angle. Am I convincing? Papa, do you see me?

Maybe, just maybe? Maybe once, if the light is just right?

Zapped! (1982)

Who would have thought that Scott Baio would play a brilliant high school–aged scientist who would conduct experiments such as one that tries to see how long mice could swim underwater if they drank Jack Daniel's? And that he'd access telekinetic powers he could use to induce women to lift up their shirts and flash him? And convince his mother that he was possessed by the devil?

I thank films like *Zapped*. Art movies usually tell us what we already know; life sentences us to loneliness and death. I need to see the unforeseeable. I need to be surprised by the world. I need to believe there is abundance. I need to know Chachi can live forever.

IV

Ten Anecdotes about the Destruction of Books

1.

I remember my friend and I throwing textbooks out the window of our third-floor high school classroom. Our Spanish teacher was senile and never noticed us leaving our desks, leaning out the windows, the stacks of extra books growing smaller and smaller.

She always seemed to have her eyes closed, rolling her r's. Or telling the class her dreams about becoming a world-famous flamenco dancer. They were well-told stories. Something that could have appeared in a good book. But we didn't care.

The joy of holding a book in our hands and watching it fall to the ground was too great.

We were always careful to make sure no one was beneath us. Once in a while we did get so excited that we failed to scan the ground below before we dropped the books. We could have really hurt someone.

Maybe such carelessness wasn't always a result of a thoughtless eagerness.

The idea of someone being clobbered with knowledge was an image we wanted to see.

2.

Living most of my childhood in a trailer park, I never owned my own books, always checking out my reading material from the public library. Because I was smart, my teachers placed me in advanced reading classes with students who had rich parents to buy whatever they wanted.

I never felt it was fair that I had to depend on an institution to supplement my education.

I wanted what everyone else had. So I stole books from the library. I'd take the book into the bathroom and rip the pages from the spine. That way I could smuggle the book out without the detector going off.

Once my friend said to me, "Why do your books always seem to fall apart so quickly?"

"Because," I said. "Anything that's loved too much falls apart."

3.

For about a year in high school I was convinced that I had a spiritual responsibility to make contact with as many people in the world as possible. There was only one problem: I was horribly shy. So I came up with a game plan: I would write notes on the inside front cover of as many library books as possible. That way I could reach people I would never meet in real life.

I remember sitting for hours and hours, writing pretentious messages in random books. I wrote things like, "To Whom This May Concern: I want you to know I have absolutely no idea who you are. But I want you to know, because I feel it's my responsibility, to tell you that you are loved. Don't turn the page of the book and begin reading because you're embarrassed someone is telling you something so obvious. It's an important thing to know no matter how reluctant you may be to accept it."

On another book I wrote, "My name is Steve Fellner. I have blond hair and blue eyes. If you're my father, please look me up in the phone book and give me a call. I miss you and want to know why you ran away from us."

4.

There was a time I was so depressed in high school that I would take a book into the bathroom with me and deliberately mishandle the pages so that I would have dozens and dozens of paper cuts. They would sting.

Then I would mumble a number of profane words at the book. Once I remember screaming at one of my mother's Harlequin romances. It looked innocent enough lying there. But I knew better. The cuts on my hands were proof of the book's guilt. I said, "How dare you cause me so much pain? You bad book. You horribly bad book."

I knew I had to punish the book. You can't let someone get away with things like that.

So I would tear off a page, crumple it up, and flush it down the toilet.

I would do that for a while. Or at least until I got bored, which was pretty quick.

5.

A girlfriend of mine in college was a theorist. She'd come over to my apartment and prefer the company of Foucault over me. I couldn't blame her. In a way. He had a lot of interesting things to say. All I wanted to do was get down her pants. I needed to prove to her that I wasn't the gay man I knew I was.

When she broke up with me, there was a stack of her library books in the corner of my room. She left me a phone message, asking if I would drop them off at the library.

I threw them all in the garbage. I remember waking up one morning before dawn to watch the garbagemen take my trash. At six in the morning they came an hour before I had begun to drink mimosas. As the truck drove away, I shouted, "To hell with insight. Where does that get you anyway?"

The next time I saw her she said that the library contacted her about overdue books. The ones I had.

"Did you return them?" she asked.

"Of course," I said. "I'm responsible."

She invited me over to her house that same week. She made me dinner. Afterward, we sat on her couch and she started to unbutton my pants. I kissed her.

"I love you," I said.

"Did you return my library books?"

"Yeah."

"Honestly," she said. "Tell me the truth. I love you."

How could I resist her?

"No," I said, "I threw them out. Don't worry. I'll pay the replacement costs."

She slapped me across the face and then told me to leave.

6.

I remember seeing my father cry for the first time. He was alone in the living room reading a book. When he saw me, he wiped away the tears, pretending nothing was going on. He folded the corner of the page he was reading. How I hated those words. Because he felt something for them he never did for me.

That same night I snuck out of my bedroom and crept down the stairs. The book was still open to that same page.

I knew I needed to do something.

I was afraid to look at the page. Let alone the cover. If it had the power to make my father cry, it might yield everlasting psychic scars for me.

So without even as much as glancing at any of the words, I tore the page from the book.

Then I sat at the kitchen table and ripped the page into little pieces.

Every night for a month I swallowed a piece.

7.

I remember one time my brother and I were so bored. Our father had deserted us. We had no idea what to do with our lives. We weren't old enough to drive so we were forced to sit around our apartment and complain to our mother. She told us to watch a movie.

"We're sick of movies," we said.

"Play a game," she said.

"We're tired of games," we said.

"Take a walk," she said.

"Our feet don't want to move," we said.

"Read a book," she said.

We couldn't stop laughing. That was our mother for you.

We stole one of Dad's sci-fi novels from her room. We tore out pages and made paper airplanes. It was so much fun. The man-made vehicles darted around the room, colliding into the furniture.

"Where'd you get that paper?" she said.

"It's Dad's," we said.

"You mean, you tore up your father's book?" she said.

We nodded.

She grabbed the book from our hands and made another airplane herself.

"Let's have a race," she said.

8.

Once my mother announced to my brother and I that she was determined to make sure that we transcended our trailer-park background. "I'm going to see to it that you guys are cultured," she said. We were nervous. Culture had always seemed so boring, especially when people invoked it in such a grand, important way.

She led us into the kitchen where there were several cookbooks lying on the table. There was one for Indian food, one for Mexican, one for Thai. My brother and I took a step backward. We were scared. We were Midwesterners who lived on a diet of casseroles and meatloaf.

"Tonight's Thai," Mother said.

For several hours she barricaded herself in the kitchen, refusing to let us in, telling us to enjoy the odors wafting our way.

The only thing we smelled that had any distinction was smoke.

Mother ran out of the kitchen, screaming for us to fetch the fire extinguisher. My brother followed her order. We put out the fire.

In a large pot, there seemed to be scorched noodles and some crusty vegetables. "Go get a manila envelope from the hall closet," Mother said.

My brother came back and held it open for her. Mother dumped the stuff in the pot and then ripped out the recipe from the book and put it inside the envelope. She told me to lick it. I did. Then she wrote the address of the publishing company on the outside. She commanded me to go slide the package into the mailbox.

I balked.

"They need to know what their recipes are capable of," she said.

I nodded and ran barefoot all the way to the box.

9.

I never wanted my parents to read me bedtime stories.

They weren't good actors. I could always tell they despised each other. They both spent so much time looking out the window, imagining their getaway car. Reading to me gave them an excuse to leave the other downstairs.

Once I said to my mother, "I'll fall asleep quicker without your words."

She insisted it was no trouble. She wanted to read to me.

One day I decided to take a magic marker and scribble out all the words to the story. When it was time for our nightly ritual, my father said, "Look what someone did to this book."

"Guess no story tonight," I said.

My father looked at me and said, "I don't want to leave yet. Would you mind just looking at the pictures?"

"I'm tired," I said.

"Please. Just give me some time. You don't need to do anything. I'll turn the pages."

10.

I've always had a hard time finishing a novel. I always lose interest midway through. I wish that this problem had to do only with books. Once my mother noticed this characteristic. "It's cruel not to finish a book," she said. "It's a form of abuse."

Assuming she was joking, I laughed.

"I'm serious," she said. "Would you just walk away from someone when they're talking to you?"

"No," I said.

"Didn't think you were like your father," she said. "You have a responsibility to let the other person say 'The End.' You shouldn't do it for them."

"I'm sorry," I said.

"Don't apologize to me," she said. "Ask the book for forgiveness."

Popsicles

I remember sitting with my mother in the common area of the dementia ward and she kept pointing to her tongue. I didn't know what she was doing. I was agitated. And I went and got a nurse. I couldn't deal with it after I got her water and it did nothing. The nurse said, "Oh, it's popsicle time." I didn't think my mother knew what was being said, but there was something in her eyes that looked elated when she heard the word *popsicle*. The nurse said, "One second. I'll be back." I didn't know whether or not to follow the nurse (wasn't it rude to be silent, essentially asking her to come back?) or sit there. If I have a choice between two possibilities, I almost always choose the one of inertia. Which is one of my many tragic flaws. I'm afraid I'll get lost somehow. Several minutes passed, and I felt bad, I felt that I was treating the nurse like a waitress, which I didn't mean to do, but I did. I took my mother's hand and there were all these elderly men and women circled around the nurse, reaching for popsicles. One almost knocked the box out of her hand. The nurse saw us and smiled and waved to another orderly who passed out the rest of the popsicles. The nurse then waved to us to go to another room and there was a little fridge. There was ice cream inside. My mother shook her head, no. She almost looked violent. The nurse you could tell was hurt: She tried

to make us feel special. I felt bad for the nurse. I felt worse
for me: I wanted the ice cream. I actually hate ice cream.
But I wanted to feel special. Like it was a celebration. And
I hated my mother at that moment. I hated her. I thought,
Just eat the fucking ice cream. The nurse started to get up,
but I said, "I'll get it." And I went and got my mother a popsicle. And then I came back and she shoved it in her mouth.
She was slurping. The nurse gave me a small bowl of chocolate ice cream. It was such a small bowl I wanted to cry. I
thought, She is going to use the rest of this ice cream on
another mother and son who will appreciate it. And when
she tells the story to someone else, maybe her own mother,
they will laugh at me and my mother who had no appreciation for the kindness. And I looked at my mother who
started to gag on the popsicle. And I thought, Serves you
right. But then a moment later, I felt bad. She looked like
she was going to throw the popsicle on the ground. And if
she did, I couldn't bear it. So I took the popsicle from her
hands and licked it. And it was better than the chocolate ice
cream. I hate chocolate. I hate ice cream. Nothing is worse
than chocolate ice cream. But I liked the popsicle. I don't
know if I actually did. But the popsicle was cold. I liked it
for that reason. It felt like it was going to burn my tongue.

On Insignificance

It took my father three years to discover I had a memoir published. It was a small gay press. But still. It was a book. It was out in the world.

My father worked for Commonwealth Edison. My friends and I called him Hipless Lew the Meter Reader. Year-round he traipsed through people's backyards, recording the numbers on the little dials attached to metal boxes. He moved from house to house fast. He knew how much energy people consumed.

He had to be exact. He often knelt on the ground and squinted. Whenever I accompanied him, which I did on and off for years, he only erased a number on his pad once. "This is the only time I've messed up," he said. "And you had to be here as a witness."

My father worked five days a week, eight-plus hours a day. After work, he always drank a Manhattan on the rocks. I never knew what the phrase "on the rocks" meant. All I knew: It sounded cool. Tough, monosyllabic, jagged.

I didn't have the strength to do a job like his. I'd be unconfident that I'd read the dial right. I would erase the numbers. I'd never hit a rhythm walking. I wobble and stumble. I never glide. In high school gym class, I never ran. I grazed. Like a stationary cow. That's what my gym teachers said: *You graze.* I took it as a compliment. For me, flattery and ridicule have the same effect: I feel spotlighted.

My father did not go to college. He was too busy chasing energy. That's the way I like to think of his job: chasing energy. He was never promoted. I remember one night walking in on him kneeling, praying, "Please don't give me a promotion. I want to be outdoors. Never behind a desk."

He's always called me a bohemian. That's how he views higher education: You move from school to school, looking for some elusive thing, called knowledge. He might be right. Each time I moved for an advanced degree (three times), I packed up my suitcase with a few books and a single change of clothes. Then I left. I carried a dog-eared copy of Jay McInerney's *Bright Lights, Big City.* Plot: A young *New Yorker* copy editor wants to write the Great American Novel. He is a promiscuous drug addict. Everyone's heard the story. It feels like a guidebook for failed MFA students. I've never read past the third page.

Strangely, or perhaps not, I believe that my father and I have the same job. He reads meters; I read books. Our observations focus on how the world behaves. We are the same. To a degree.

*

Like most middle-aged gay men, I spent a good deal of my childhood in the closet. It's an embarrassing fact. After I came out, I feared AIDS. Funerals and lesions. Those were the spectacles of my teenage years. I saw my first lesion on a boyfriend's arm. It looked like a tattoo of a purple rose. It was gorgeous. When we were in bed, I sniffed it. I like beautiful things.

My father's response to me telling him I was gay: "Don't die of AIDS. I'd be bummed." For Christmas, he gave me a

Chippendales calendar. "Now you don't need to have sex," he wrote in a card. "Jerk off. When you're bored, change months. There's always more time and more guys." I accepted his words as poetry. Once he laughed when I told him I remembered our talk about the birds and bees. "Yes," I said, "it's haunted me." This is how it began: "Son, do you know what tits are?" That is also how it ended.

*

My memoir doesn't include much about my father. It includes a time my parents and their best friends drunkenly played a game of Truth or Dare. As the game went on, my parents told too much truth: They didn't love each other. They wanted a divorce.

It includes my indebtedness to him for taking me to art movies. He used to laugh at how serious everyone looked when they left the theatre. His response most often: "It wasn't *that* boring." It includes his relationship with the woman he met after the divorce. It includes the lifelong dreams he forgot and never remembered. I wrote about him in a measured and reasonable way. Perhaps that's why I feared he'd be upset: It made him look human, exactly like everybody else.

*

So, after graduating with a PhD in creative writing (how embarrassing!), and landing a job, my memoir was published. I never told him. Not a thing. It sounds weirder than what it was.

I went through my degree programs. He never asked about school. I never told him.

I don't think I ever used the word *artist* with my father. *That* did sound bohemian. But I do wonder if my father ever denied his artistic ambitions. Last time I visited him in Florida, I noticed that he began to trace paintings. There were landscapes and portraits and still lifes. He even tried the *Mona Lisa*. There was something touching in trying to replicate every stroke, every brush, every line. For me, that's a love of art. When I compliment him, he's embarrassed. "All I do is trace history," he said. I didn't have the courage to tell him the truth: That's all creative nonfiction does, too.

*

A small grassroots press published my book. They were starting out. They didn't even know what an ISBN was. They were good people. I pushed them to sell it on Amazon, which isn't cheap as it steals all the profits. Oprah wasn't going to select it for her book club. Even though they paid all the submission fees, I wasn't going to win a Pulitzer Prize. No, my book would be the smallest blip imaginable, which means no one would ever know it existed. This was fine with me. What right did I have to even write a memoir? Who am I?

I received one favorable review in a city paper and the Lambda website. That was it, more or less. If you Google me now, nothing'll show up. I'm not embarrassed. I put a book in the world. As a teacher said to me, "Creating is better than not creating." I don't know if that's true, but it sounds nice.

And then three years after the book was published, after I had gotten married, after I had two bipolar episodes, after my husband became ill, after my mother was diagnosed with uterine cancer and dementia, after all that, my father called to tell me he had read the book.

The message was on my voicemail: "YOU WROTE A BOOK ABOUT OUR LIVES AND YOU DIDN'T EVEN FUCKING TELL ME!"

*

My father doesn't understand how Amazon works, which is understandable. He assumes all books are equal in the world. At astounding rates, memoirs, no matter how insignificant, are being bought and sold. After all, it is on a website everyone knows about, including him, someone who never reads. It was hard to explain that most things go unnoticed. I imagined him at home, frantically typing *Fellner,* seeing there were a few copies, purchasing them, hoping that would stop people from finding out our dull secrets.

It took him a second to realize what an Amazon sales rank is. And how you can determine no one is buying your book. When he understood, he felt guilty. "Maybe if I was a more interesting person, your book would have been a blockbuster."

He compared and contrasted the number of pages he appeared in against other friends and family. He answered his own question.

He theorized that I loved my mother more than him. "That's the good thing about reading meters," he said. "You accept a number tells you everything."

*

My father offered a number of early childhood memories that were curiously missing from the book: him coming up with the title of my first short story ("The Meaning of Life"); him buying me my favorite writing utensil (Hello Kitty ballpoint pen); him driving me to a high school creative writing awards assembly at Harper Community College (won for a collection of movie reviews for movies he took me to).

*

Of course, the question he wanted to know I never answered: Why did I not tell him?

I didn't know exactly either.

I never feared he would accuse me of making things up. Even though he never said the memoir was 100% true, he never said any of it was false. He said, "There's a kernel of truth in every scene." For me, that was more than enough validation.

Perhaps I was afraid of him reading it and then saying, "That's all?" I'd say yes. And then he'd say OK. And there'd be nothing more to say.

Perhaps I was afraid of him saying he wasn't a three-dimensional character. Perhaps I was afraid he was right. One of my most significant flaws as an essayist: If I'm not careful, I transform real-life people into caricatures of themselves. There are scenes where I make my father aloof and blinded. His own survival is a result of obliviousness. I make him cartoonish, like a Mr. Magoo.

Which isn't fair. I write essays like Mr. Magoo. I can still remember the episodes where the cartoon character stumbles into a construction site, some sort of dangerous setting. Practically blind, he manages to find safety after stumbling on rickety beams, trembling on half-finished stairs, surviving random pulleys and levers. That's me drafting an essay. Never clear-sighted, I fumble and flail until I somehow find a way to the end of a draft.

*

Or perhaps worst of all, after I finished my memoir, I felt that my life was reclaimed and all mine. All mine. I didn't want to share it with anyone.

*

There weren't any recriminations or much fallout. I hear from a number of writers that when their family read their memoir, a vicious brawl ensued. Over the years, my family has become less aggressive. With most of our conflicts, anger dissipates quickly, not because of an essential goodness, but it's tiring (and boring) to remain angry at someone. There's always new, more significant calamities to face.

Was I disappointed that there wasn't going to be a series of screaming matches and threatening lawsuits? Maybe.

Maybe I feared that if friends and family agreed that the memoir was at least a moderately skilled blueprint of our lives, nothing more, it would be the ultimate condemnation: There was nothing worthy of a memoir. No secrets to reveal. No consequences except one angry phone call.

The Pencil Box

In high school, my best friend Abigail was always holding a pencil box. It was neon pink. A small dent on the right-hand side. Even then, she called herself an artist, which irritated me. If you came from a trailer park, as we did, you don't attach labels like that to yourself. It was silly. You needed to work hard. People who work hard don't carry pencil boxes.

The pencil box troubled me. She looked vulnerable. Her pencils mattered to her. I feared someone would steal the pencil box. If they had, I feared she wouldn't become what I wanted to be: an artist.

I remembered once walking with my mother down a street and someone coming up from behind, snatching her purse. She didn't run after the man. She dropped to her knees and cried. I hated her. Parents should always protect their kids from seeing true vulnerability.

A purse can contain valuable items like money, makeup kit, condoms. There is an expected and understandable loss when it's stolen. A pencil box only carries pencils. Pencils aren't valuable. You can walk out of your house and go to a convenience store and buy pencils. No big deal. For me, the most tragic losses are the most insignificant. You receive comfort from people if someone snatches your purse. No one cares if someone stole your pencil box. True tragedy is when no one sees the crime.

Perhaps this is what bothered me the most about the pencil box. It meant she had decided to become an artist. She had purchased something that said to the world, "I need to write. I have a pencil to write. I am an artist who writes."

That pencil box was taunting me. It said, "You don't want to commit to anything. You will never be anything more than a kid lost in a trailer park."

Abigail never wore nice clothes. They were always disheveled. My mother worked at an office where people learned how to apply for jobs. They were given free nice clothes to wear to an interview. Work clothes were expensive. Once my mother asked me if I wanted to give Abigail a dress. I said, no, if she wore one nice dress, it might make her want another nice dress. I didn't want to turn her greedy.

I wondered if Abigail would have chosen to keep her pencil box over having a lot of new nice dresses. I never asked her.

What also upset me: She wasn't embarrassed about holding onto a pencil box all day long. She didn't seem to care what anyone else thought. Sure, people say that all the time, even me on a rare occasion, but she truly did not care. She was too young. She needed to be punished for having the confidence to ignore everyone else. Once someone told me that the good thing about old age, not youth, was that you ignored what everyone else thought.

Here was Abigail, a mere high schooler, and she had the intelligence of an ancient person. It didn't seem fair. I started to dream about that pencil box. As in real life, it was always pink. I dreamt that the pencil box fell to the ground and as Abigail went to pick it up, I tried to stomp on it. But nothing happened. God decided the pencil box was too important. He wouldn't let me ruin it.

Once I asked Abigail if I could borrow the pencil box.
She looked as confused as I was. Who borrows such a thing?
You can ask someone for a pencil in the box. But not the
box itself.

Strangely, I realized I never saw her take a pencil out of
the box. Or anything else. The pencil box was like a gift she
didn't want to ruin through opening it.

I had no choice. I had to steal the box. One day after class,
I went up to her on the playground. It was one of those rare
times the pencil box was in her backpack. I said, "You need
to go into the principal's office now. Something happened to
your mom."

She was so anxious she couldn't find her bag. "It's here," I
said, holding it. "I'll hold it for you. Run."

Of course, I took the pencil box.

The principal and Abigail came to the playground. He was
not happy. "Who lied to you and said Abigail needed to see
if her mother was dying?"

"I don't know," I said. "Some kids in the hall were saying
it."

He believed me. I was an excellent student.

At home, I ran to my room and closed the door. For some
reason, I expected magic inside, which is a silly thing to
think, even at that age. But I did. I took a deep breath.

There was a folded note. It was from her father. It said:
Keep this letter. You'll never receive another.

I went into the bathroom, tore it up and flushed it down
the toilet. Threw the pencil box into the kitchen garbage.

*

I never got caught, which at the time, felt right. Abigail cheated me. I didn't want a personal letter to be in the pencil box. But I didn't want pencils inside, either. It didn't seem fair. I deserved more. More importantly, she deserved more.

I'm not sure what more I wanted for her. All I knew was that what we received felt like less. A lot less. A week later, Abigail had a new pencil box. She didn't even mention the old one.

The new pencil box was blue. Red stripes. For a second, it looked completely different. Then after a day or two of watching her hold it, it didn't.

On Love, Sex, and
Thom Gunn

1.

At the queer kiss-in no one wanted to make out with me. It took place in the college union. Everyone immediately paired up. I wondered if it was correct in describing a kiss-in as activism. It seemed like one should suffer (at least a little) in their fight for justice. Then again, what did I know? I was a dumb, just-out-of-the-closet undergrad.

I called up the president of the Gay and Lesbian Alliance. "Should activism be enjoyable?" I said.

There was a long silence. "Were you the guy alone in the corner?"

"I was hugging myself," I said. "I was making a political statement."

Once I started openly doubting the merits of the kiss-in, he said that a suicidal freshman had just come into the office. He had to go take care of them. They needed his help. I told him I'd wait for him to call me back. He said sure. I never heard from him.

The next day I walked over to his office. "What's your major?" he said.

"English."

He grabbed a book from his shelf and handed it to me. "You're not an activist. Next time there's a kiss-in you should stay home and read."

2.

He gave me a poetry book called *The Man with Night Sweats.* It was written by Thom Gunn. As far as I know, it's the first collection that contains a series of formal poems that deal with gay male suffering in the AIDS pandemic.

Most of the poems rhyme. I hate rhyme. It might have been fine when Keats was alive, but after that, it was time to get over it. I imagine Keats, a young, sick man, looking at himself in the mirror, saying words aloud, almost singing, listening for that perfect sound. I'm sure he looked good doing it.

But I don't like pretty things. I always want to bust them wide open.

3.

After reading *The Man with Night Sweats,* I decided I wanted to become a poet. But there were things I wanted to avoid. I found that a good number of openly gay poets were strict traditionalists in form and content. Unlike heterosexual writers, it seemed that you had to prove yourself in a way they didn't.

Queer poets (and prose writers) employed so many mythological and biblical allusions. An intricate familiarity with canonical texts seemed to be required before you could move onto your own metaphors. You had to show that you weren't going to go rogue. You needed to obey the traditions established. You needed to show that you were a good, dutiful queer.

4.

During my undergraduate years, there was only one gay and lesbian literature class offered. I was the first one to sign up.

I fell in love with the guy who sat in the front row. I always liked students who sat up close. They were good people who believed what they were told. Their brains were empty and needed to be filled up with the right ideas. That's why they sat so close. They couldn't risk knowledge losing its way.

Also, would a straight guy sit in the front of class? Wouldn't someone who was heterosexual want to keep their distance? Why risk being labeled as queer? Then again, what kind of man would even take a queer literature class? It was the early '90s. Things were different back then.

I told my best friend I had a crush on the guy in the front row. "I love him," I said.

I liked throwing the word *love* around. It felt transgressive and edgy. It gave me a charge. My friend told me I should write him a note. I did. She took it and gave it to the student who sat in front of her. Who gave it to the student who sat in front of him. And so on . . .

He came up to me after class and said, "Hey, buddy, I'm straight. Or else I would date you in a second." I swooned.

A few days later I saw him walking down the quad, holding another man's hand.

5.

That gay male lit teacher rarely assigned any poetry. One day I approached him after class and asked why.

"Who would you want me to put on the syllabus?" he asked.

"Thom Gunn," I said. I couldn't think of another name.

"If he had been a halfway decent fuck, he might have ended up on it."

6.

It might sound unbelievable that I never looked at gay porn until college. Perhaps it's because my mother owned hundreds of used Harlequin romance novels. Every square inch of our trailer was lined with them. There were even some in the bottom basket of the refrigerator. Our place was small. She had to take advantage of every spot for storage.

I never opened one of the books. All I did was look at the covers. Invariably, they were all the same: Muscular shirtless men adorned them. They all had big pecs and Fabio-like hair. I was in love. (Even if I found the hair and the over-muscled body somewhat repulsive. As I do now.)

But this is my point: Everywhere in my home was jack-off material. I didn't realize all these men were gazing at me. I should have felt loved.

7.

One particularly lonely night, I grabbed *The Man with Night Sweats* from my bedside table. It felt good to read depictions of gay men dying, their lovers wrecked with loss, family members destroyed, hospital workers disgusted on occasion. Thinking about poems made me feel better. Reading stuff about AIDS saved me from depression. People were in worse shape than me.

But then, the next day, I started to imagine how happy the men had been before the disease hit. I imagined them in alleyways and bathhouses and forests and spas. I imagined them being as carefree as possible. I imagined them throwing me up against a wall and saying, "Open up."

And then I imagined myself dying. Alone. The dying isn't what bothered me. The aloneness did. I've always wanted a crowd to witness my death.

8.

Sometimes I tried picking up guys in bathrooms. I took books with explicitly gay covers inside. Put them on a stack on the floor and sat on the toilet seat. I hoped a gay man would come in and see them. Once someone in the stall next to me started tapping their foot. My cock got hard. He slid his foot underneath the wall. I was annoyed. I didn't know why. That's what I wanted him to do.

I exited the stall. He recognized the cover. He grabbed the book and said, "Look at this." I was impressed. The poem was about Gunn picking up someone in the bathroom.

"Meta, no?" he said.

I raised my hand like I was going to hit him. "Get the fuck out of here," I said. "Before I call the police and have you arrested."

9.

Prose is always hard for me to write. Too many words. You need to spend a lot of time at the computer. You can't just dash something off like you can a poem. Bad prose doesn't fool people as often as bad poems. That's why I went into graduate school as a poet: less work. I wanted to have sex a lot. I didn't want anything to get in the way.

I was still often frustrated with my limitations as a writer. After I finished a series of poems, I realized how weak they were and threw them away. When this happened, I became depressed and picked up a man. Once after working for an inordinately long time on some poems, I realized that my work was worse than flawed; it was completely inept and dumb. Upon this assessment, I had the immediate urge to go have public sex. I found someone in a restroom. I came on the wall. I didn't clean it up. I left and went home to bed. I slept for three days, too depressed and exhausted to shave or put on clothes. All my energy was focused on one detail: I wanted to know if anyone cleaned up after me.

I wanted to have left a mark.

10.

As a graduate student, I wanted to be cool. So: I dated someone who was HIV-positive. His name was Bill. Bill was a wonderful cook, so I convinced him to throw dinner parties for our friends. We had at least one dinner party a week. Somehow during the conversation I always made sure we talked about AIDS. I made a huge speech about how people with AIDS are misrepresented, shut out of health care, etc. Later during the night I whispered to anyone who I suspected didn't know that Bill was HIV-positive, that he had contracted the disease years ago, that I knew that going into the relationship, and that it didn't bother me at all. "We're all going to end up in hell anyway," I joked. Everyone looked sufficiently impressed. I was pleased with myself.

Bill and I never had sex. Once when he started to kiss my neck, I said, "Get away from me, you know you have that disease."

He threatened to leave me. So I started crying. He made it up to me by throwing a large dinner party for my friends.

Seven whole courses. Homemade pasta. During the meal, I talked about how people needed to stop fearing their bodies and learn to let go a little. In front of everyone, I kissed Bill on the lips.

11.

When Bill and I were in bed together, I prayed that he would talk in his sleep. It's not like I expected him to say something deep. I wanted him to say something that *could be interpreted* as profound. I wanted him to say something that I could claim was found poetry.

12.

It was boring watching a man die of AIDS. "From my end of things, it's dullsville, too," Bill said.

I expected us to do a lot of screaming, carrying on about our love for one another. But we didn't. We snapped. I pouted when I had to wipe up his vomit off the bathroom floor. But I didn't even really mind that. In fact, I enjoyed it. Cleaning up after him gave me something to do. It was like we were waiting each other out.

We talked about our "dream" deaths. Mine was dying of natural causes. He wanted to be buried alive. The thought of himself scratching at the wooden lid of the coffin six feet undergrou'nd amused him. He knew he'd run out of air. But he could choose when he was going to die. Conserve air, or indulge and take deep breaths. It was all up to him. Sooner or later.

13.

Bill and I went to see a fortune teller. It wasn't my sort of thing, but he insisted. "I'm dying," he said. "You have to do what I say."

It sounded like a reasonable claim.

The fortune teller looked restless and bored. I opened my hands so she could read my palms, but she waved them away.

"I don't like to touch my clients," she said. "Too intimate. Ask me a question."

She then turned to Bill.

"If you dream you're dead, does that mean you're going to die?" Bill asked.

"Yes," the fortune teller said. "It means soon. It will happen soon. Prepare."

"I thought it meant you're just entering a rebirth?" I said.

"Those are lies," she said. "To make your final days bearable."

14.

When my boyfriend Bill finally died of AIDS, I was oddly relieved, almost happy. Now I could be a writer. I had a subject. No one would take that away from me.

Although Bill had tried to. Before he died, he said, "I know you don't really love me. You want to be a writer. You're here for one reason: My dying is good material."

"Nice to know you see me as a saint," I said.

"No problem," he said. "And just so you know: There's a lot of people writing about this stuff. Better writers than you. By the time you get the skill to do it, it'll be too late. Dying boyfriend with lesions will be a huge cliché."

It was true. The day he died I tried to write an elegy in formal verse. It included all the clichés: hospital visits, bitchy humor, wistful sexual remembrances. They read like the worst sort of derivatives of Thom Gunn.

I still blamed my inability in writing a successful AIDS elegy on Thom Gunn. I hated him. And Mark Doty. And Rafael Campo. And Paul Monette. And John Ashberry. And Reginald Shepherd. And Mark Wunderlich. And Henri Cole. And J. D. McClatchy. And David Trinidad. And D. A. Powell. And Essex Hemphill. And Tim Dlugos. And Timothy Liu. And Richard McCann. And so on and so on. There wasn't enough room for all these men and me to love the same men, the same disease.

15.

For this essay, I decided not to use any quotations from Thom Gunn's poems. I didn't want his poems to upstage my prose. Dear Reader, I don't want you to love him more than me. And this isn't a tribute. Or a scholarly article. And it definitely isn't a love letter. To anyone.

16.

Prior to the release of my debut book of poems, I thought it would be good to gather advance interest in my writings. So: I created a blog. It was called Pansy Poetics. When people start a blog, they often post their own work. I didn't. No poet wants to read another poet's work. They have better things to do. Like create their own poems.

But I did know that I would attract a readership if I attacked a beloved gay poet's work. Of course, Thom Gunn was off-limits. But another popular poet/essayist wasn't. I wrote a triptych of posts about his work, confessing a tortured ambivalence to his writings. Because he is popular, I knew that anything less than a wholly favorable response would cause some people to react. I was right.

Some people said that you should never criticize people in your own community, especially if that group of people was often under siege. I understood their point. But I didn't care.

Some of the worst damage in my life has been caused by other gay men, not heterosexuals. You can always dismiss the homophobes. But when one of your own rips you, you know something is probably definitely wrong.

17.

Perhaps the elegy is most susceptible to a dishonorable sentimentality. When I read through *The Man with Night Sweats*, I was annoyed at how all the AIDS victims seemed to be good people. Everyone was angelic, or innocent, or caring. In fact, I started to wonder about Thom Gunn himself: Why did he hang around such boring people? I imagined himself rolling his eyes at the buff jock at the gym (even if he wanted to fuck him). Or the trendy gay men who cared more about their accessories than their philosophies. Or the self-righteous allies who might have pledged support at the bar but were nowhere to be found at the rallies, hospital rooms.

18.

One of my friends came home to his apartment to find his lover and his best friend in bed. My friend kicked them out and called me on the phone. "It all comes down to who you love," my friend said to me. "When you love a man you're doomed. The man will cheat. It's inevitable."

"There's forms of betrayal other than cheating physically with someone else," I said. "That's just usually the easiest to identify."

"Don't be a Pollyanna."

"Not at all," I said. "I'm just saying that everyone betrays their lover in some way."

"Then how do you know if he ever loved you?"

"It's a question of not who loved you, but how you loved. All that matters is how tortured your lover is when he's found out. If they express shame and regret, then they've done the most they can for you. Then they've loved you."

19.

Over the years, my affinity with Thom Gunn has waned. I became obsessed with the gay poet James Schuyler. He won the Pulitzer Prize. Am I offering my affection to someone who has already received enough love from the poetry establishment? Thom Gunn never did receive arguably the most prestigious award in the realm of literature.

James Schuyler wrote in a self-admittedly diaristic way. Everything was of the moment. He often wrote in the present tense. He populates his poems with real people and events. Essentially, everything is true. He has a casual style. You never feel like he's trying to write poems that will last forever. No ego. His poems are almost always infused or at least tinged with a serious pastoral element.

I like his poems so much that I wrote one for him. It was published. It's called *Ode to James Schuyler*. Here's the poem in its entirety:

I cruise
your poems for the names
of pharmaceuticals.

Entertaining to think I might
be on the same stuff
as my idol.

Nowhere do I see
a diagnosis though.
Too many flowers blocking

the view. Madonna
lilies, lemon mint,
hyacinths, Old China

Monthly Rose,
etc., etc.
I can't see over them.

I never wrote a poem for Thom Gunn. The thought never
occurred to me.

20.

Whenever I attend a Q&A with a visiting writer, I ask them
if they believe in ghosts. Most of them look a little shocked.
I can't tell if it's because they're relieved that I didn't ask the
usual sort of questions: What made you realize you wanted
to be a writer? What's your routine? Who are your literary idols? Have you read anything that you liked lately that
deserves a shout-out?

None of that. I ask them if they believe in ghosts.

I don't trust people who refuse to have faith in the other-worldly. For me, that's what poetry should do: capture what isn't visible. To capture the spirit. To capture the texture of someone's soul.

To my surprise, I sometimes receive emotional responses: "Words are real. I am real. I'm interested in the real."

Or: "I'm a poet. Not a Ghostbuster."

And: "I've always wanted to be on *Celebrity Ghost Stories.* Got any connections?"

To which I replied: "Can a poet ever be a celebrity?"

21.

Which I suppose is an unfair question: If they say yes, they'll look like an egomaniac. If they say no, they look unambitious, comfortable with their own mediocrity.

How many people need to acknowledge you to be a celebrity?

If enough fans purchase your book that you need a second or third printing, does that constitute celebrity status? If MFA students can push your Amazon sales rank up to the double digits? If your friends and family don't lie to you and actually do read your book?

Or how about just one, a bespectacled, geeky librarian? What if she glances at your poem in a journal and reads a single poem from start to finish and commits your name to memory—even if she forgets it a few seconds later?

22.

I bet Thom Gunn considered himself a celebrity. If so, I hoped he took advantage of that status as much as he could and fucked every overeager young grad student. (This is not a personal fantasy of mine. Anyone under the age of thirty-five bores me.)

I found an old video of him giving a reading. You can tell the audience is impressed with his British accent. And his self-deprecation. And his claim Jeffrey Dahmer inspired several poems. And then a surprise linkage between Dahmer and Christopher Marlowe.

He's saying all the right things, making leaps in unexpected ways. His own introductions to his poems embody everything the poems refuse to be: messy, funny, askew. I find myself fast-forwarding through the poems to listen to his bantering. I like seeing his face more than reading his poems.

23.

To write an elegiac poem is to engage in necrophilia. You are caressing words to enliven the body of your beloved.

24.

When I first started teaching, I always said to my students: *Avoid sentimentality at all costs.* This isn't particularly effective. But I like to sound like an absolutist when I teach, maybe even when I write. It fools me into thinking I'm an authority of something.

At the same time, as a creative writing teacher, you often receive the same material: dead grandmothers, dead friends from a car accident, a dead pet animal. The protagonists of these pieces almost always shed one tear. Not several. One and only one. I don't know if that's melodrama or restraint.

25.

There might be only two poems I truly think are spectacular in Thom Gunn's book. When I realize this, I feel shame: Am I overrating the aesthetic/political merits of *The Man with Night Sweats?* One of my creative writing teachers once said, "If you really only end up loving one poem in a whole book, it's an undeniable success. How many miracles do you expect from one person?"

26.

Through the title *The Man with Night Sweats,* Thom Gunn creates an image of pity—a homosexual suffering in bed, which is emblematic of the AIDS crisis. At the same time, Thom Gunn doesn't mention the more graphic symptoms of the AIDS-impacted body such as lesions, etc.

Gay writers always need to play their cards right for acceptance. Sometimes things look too gay. Or not gay enough. You need to flatter the audience if you want their love. I called my first book *Blind Date with Cavafy.* I wanted to make a literary allusion to the famous Greek poet. If a manuscript screener studied poetry, there could be a good chance they might know this queer touchstone. People like to think their education paid off. Put that with some comedy—the idea of a blind date—and you have something, which is hip and even maybe a little edgy.

A title matters. A title can matter more than the poems.

27.

You should never write an elegy for someone before they are dead.

It's a curse. I've cursed many people.

28.

Blind Date with Cavafy won a contest. It grabbed the Thom Gunn Gay Male Poetry Award from the Publishing Triangle. It felt uncanny. Was Thom Gunn telepathic? I'd never met him. From the grave, had he sensed me obsessing over his poems throughout the years and fixed the competition so he could salute my dedication to him?

My poems have nothing in common with his. They have no sense of music: no iambic pentameter, no rhyme schemes, no formal constraints whatsoever. There is no evidence of a lineage between my aesthetics and Thom Gunn's. Except for the fact we're two queers who roamed the earth.

29.

Codependent chubby geeks, my husband Phil and I are. On the weekdays, we grade papers and botch home delivery meal kits. During the weekends, we watch obscure horror films and drink margaritas. We're quite busy. We do chat about our eventual deaths and who will suffer more. I tell him that I'll buy a big fluffy dog to replace him. He says that he'll just turn up the TV louder when I'm gone.

We like to talk about the future engravings on our tombstones. He wants his to read: "For Heaven's Sake." I want: "Please."

30.

My husband I coedited a social justice poetry anthology, which brought together new and already established writers. We wanted to include only living writers. We wanted the anthology to be as much of *the now* as it could be.

After a decade, we revisited the anthology. We noticed that several of the writers had died: one of a heart attack, one of AIDS, one of old age, one we weren't sure of. Maybe suicide. We don't know.

One of the dead poets I loved. He gave his final reading at my university. He complained about how the organizers tried to cheat him out of money. I loved that he was petty. When you're dying, you can be as petty as you want. It's only fair. He couldn't read a poem all the way through without coughing. This didn't stop him from putting on some music, doing the merengue, and getting the audience on their feet. Two faculty members were offended. "This isn't how you give a reading," they said.

It felt like the happiest funeral I've ever attended.

31.

My husband holds several lifetime grudges against me. The first: For years, I ate his secret stash of peanut butter. I swore on our lives I didn't do it. I convinced him it must be something supernatural. The second: When we first started dating, I bought him and my mother the same Valentine's Day card and wrote the same inscription. (Creepy.) The third: I never redeemed myself by writing him a love poem.

So: I did. I published a love poem for Phil. I made it clear that it was for him and only him. It was called "Love Poem for Phil." (I didn't want him to think the poem was doing double duty.) Here's the poem in its entirety:

Who else could make
my trips to the psych ER

feel like first dates? Afterwards
we always visited

Friendly's,
binged on hot fudge

sundaes. Two
apiece! Good thing

major depression takes
away a few pounds. Egads!

See the exclamation
marks. Those

are for you. I promise:
there's more where

those came from.

32.

Before I started writing this essay, I looked up everything I could find on Thom Gunn. I discovered that *A New Selected Poems* had just been released in 2019. From the prestigious Farrar Strauss & Giroux. He died in 2004. Fifteen years later, the world is still talking about him: He matters.

Maybe this essay does then, too.

33.

On Thom Gunn's *A New Selected Poems,* the cover photo
makes him looks like a second-rate 1970s porn star. Short,
slightly tousled black hair, smoldering eyes, blue jean shirt,
unbuttoned to show some chest hair. But not too far down.
You want to leave something to the imagination.

34.

Perhaps that is one of my greatest life tragedies: I've left
too much of my life to my imagination. Rather than doing,
I've been seduced by books, by the personalities of authors
I've never met. For so many years, I went to poetry readings
and promised myself I would talk to the author one-on-one
after. I never did. I ran home. I didn't want them to be different than the way I imagined them. It would have felt like
a betrayal.

I remember a gay male poet who wrote a series of poems
about a man named Ricardo. Everyone in the audience was
curious about the aftermath of the breakup. I was, too. The
poems obsessed me. I cared so much. I imagined myself giving the poet a hug after the reading. I wanted to say, "Thank
you for living a life I never had the courage to lead." Someone
in the audience asked the writer a question about Ricardo.

The author was furious. He didn't exist, he said. A wave
of sadness fell over the audience. He expressed shock someone would begin to think there was a Ricardo. He emphasized he was a *creative* writer. "My job is to make things up,"
he said.

I wanted to say to him, "Be calm. You are such a good writer that we all imagined ourselves in your world. We were there and we wanted to be. Don't take that away."

This is a shameful thing to admit: Over the years, I have gone to many friends' funerals (and avoided many as well). I rarely felt as much loss as I did with Ricardo. On my way home from the reading, I cried about him. I was bereft.

Mad Max

His name was Mad Max. The preacher's name was Mad Max. I never found out if the students gave him the name Mad Max or if he created it himself. Neither would surprise me. Each possibility is filled with pathos. If I cared about the man, I'd be upset. I don't know if he's dead. I don't even care enough to try to find out.

When I began my undergraduate career at the University of Illinois, Mad Max was one of the first people I met. I was a lonely closeted young gay man. It was the early '90s. A lot of times I roamed around the Quad by myself. I'd carry my books in my backpack, but I rarely took them out and studied. They were nothing more than props. If I passed a familiar person—someone from one of my classes or a kid from my dorm—I'd take the books out of my bag and pretend I was reading. I didn't want anyone to think I had no friends. I had some pride.

Once I strolled across the Quad and heard a man shouting things in a loud and crazed fashion. Was he yelling at me? I thought I had heard the word *homosexual,* or *sodomite,* or *cocksucker,* but I figured I was just paranoid. I hadn't told anyone I was gay.

Bible verses, all garbled, punctuated his rant. One came out after another in impressive rapid succession. He looked like a homeless man, his clothes ripped, unwashed, his beard untrimmed. He wore an odd fedora hat. There were about 100 students circled around him, screaming back. Questioning him. Calling him names. Telling him he was disgusting.

The man shouted back.

It was a creepy sight. It was like something you'd see in those gladiator movies. Imagine a big beast of a man fighting some puny heroes. Every time one of the small ones hits and slashes the monster's body, the crowd cheers, yelping for more and more. Your witnessing can't help but make you feel a little dizzy.

No doubt the man was mentally ill.

I didn't care about that fact. I didn't care about the cruelty of the students. I really didn't. I'm not going to pretend to have been ashamed.

There was only one thing that held (and still holds) any interest: It was said that before this ill man became Mad Max, the preacher on the Quad, he had been a well-respected college professor.

*

I always knew I wanted to be a professor. When I was a kid, I was obsessed with worksheets, any subject, math, science, history, etc. I can still remember asking my third-grade teacher if I could have whatever xeroxed ones were left over so I could redo them at home. Workbooks were also a great joy. I loved racing through the pages, going as quickly as I could, filling out blank after blank. Those blanks were my best friends. I could make them whole, worth something.

*

At the age of thirty-six, I became suicidal. Weeks before I started to complete my tenure application, I went mad.

The symptoms of my nervous breakdown were unremarkable. Most of my life is nothing special, nothing worthy of a memoir, any sort of personal essay. This is what happened before my full-fledged emotional collapse, culminating in a diagnosis of bipolar disorder: I started to feel out of breath all the time. I would become so sweaty and overheated that I would put my head between my legs and pray to God that I wouldn't die. For days, I went sleepless. I was convinced that there were people in my life who wanted to hurt me personally and professionally. (I still don't think that's entirely false.) My husband Phil took me to the emergency room and they did MRIs. No problems there. There was nothing abnormal in the blood tests either.

Everything was in my head. I called up Sam, a best friend, and told her that I wanted to cut off my hands. It was a strange, obsessive thought. I couldn't get anything done except thinking about the advantages in cutting off my hands.

Sam handled me quite well. "I don't think that would be a good idea," she said.

"They're just such hindrances."

"Sometimes they are," she said. "But they're worth the bother. Why don't you keep them around for a little bit longer? At least until you see a shrink."

She sounded like she knew what she was talking about. I took her advice.

*

I've always been a bit agoraphobic. When I was an undergraduate, there was only one reason I left my dorm room: my roommates. It didn't bother me that they were Christians who hosted Bible studies both Friday and Saturday night.

This was the problem: They never stopped watching *The Blues Brothers*. I still know almost every line from that movie by heart. They would stay up until 5 a.m. watching it for the umpteenth time, their pleasure never lacking.

I spent even more time on the Quad, always ending up making my way to Mad Max. I never talked to him. He had too many people surrounding him.

Once a female classmate approached me. "You want to talk to him, don't you?

"Yes," I said. "I want him to know not everybody hates him."

"That's what I wanted," she said. "The other day I went up and tried to have a conversation."

"What did he say?"

"He called me a cunt."

*

When I was an undergraduate, I majored in English. I was never one to go to a teacher's office hours. I had nothing to say. I was an OK writer. I received all A's. My strength: I turned things in on time.

Once a teacher gave me a C. I was upset. I decided to go talk to her. Her office was on the fifth floor. It was quite a walk. When I knocked on her door, she was obviously happy.

"I just found out I got tenure," she said. "I'm set for life. Nothing can get me now. Why are you here?"

"You gave me a C."

She took out her grade book and penned a large A+ next to my name. "Time to blow this pop stand," she said.

She opened her desk drawer and took out a box of cookies. "Follow me," she said.

She raced down the stairs and then walked toward Mad Max. He was shouting as usual. I stayed several feet away from him. I could still smell his odor. She offered him the box of cookies. He took it.

"You always want to be kind to permanent neighbors," she said.

*

When I was a graduate student in Syracuse, I agreed to meet a man at a coffee shop. We had been regularly talking online. He was a psychology professor. Our chats included him telling me that he had come out of the closet when he was forty. He told his wife, who was very kind. She was sad and angry, but she worked through it. In fact, after a few months, she said, "I've just got to learn to love you in a different way."

I arrived at the coffee shop half an hour early. I waited for the man who described himself as fit and trim, quite put together, albeit not the best dresser. The man turned out to be seriously overweight. Which was not a big deal: People lie about their weight and age all the time.

I know I did.

What concerned me was that this man seemed unhinged. He sat down and started chewing his fingernails. His shirt had a stain on it, his hair was unkempt.

I figured he must have been lying about being a teacher. Literary and psychoanalytic theory have a lot in common. I tried to engage him in a conversation about Lacan and Freud. He immediately picked up the threads. He knew more than me. I couldn't stop.

"You're not attracted to me, are you?" he said.

"You don't look well."

We drank our coffee and went to his car. His back window was cracked. Everything was a mess inside. When we got in the car, he started shaking.

"I think I'm having a breakdown," he said. He then gave me black rosary beads and said, "You can't help me. Maybe these can help you some day."

I have them in a coffee mug on my desk at the university where I work. I only recently have begun to forget they are there.

*

No one ever abandoned me when I told them I was gay. It was no big deal. Two of my closest friends turned their backs on me when I was sick. One was a wife of a faculty member. She was a very attractive woman who worked in a mental institution. She never talked about her job. I saw this as an honorable act; it's not good to reveal other people's secrets. Once she told me that an inmate snuck past her and ended up escaping. He only managed to stay hidden for a few hours. It seemed to be no big deal even though it was on the news.

For several weeks, whenever she came to pick me up in her car, I started crying once I got inside. She said to me, "If you're depressed, don't worry. It'll go away. Just don't let anyone put you on meds. All that will happen is you'll be tired all the time and get fat."

"I'm always tired and fat."

"Good point," she said. "It looks like you don't have much to worry about."

*

I always wonder if Mad Max had friends, and how many. He must have had at least two or three in the department. There can be no doubt about that, can there? Someone should have seen what was going on and saved him.

I imagine his best friend—I don't know why, but I see her as a woman—seeing him become more and more withdrawn, closing the door to his office with greater regularity. I imagine him always anticipating going out for drinks with her after a hard day of work and then slowly saying no, he really had too much to do, really, he would if he could, but not now, not at this moment. I imagine her going to see the department head, expressing her concern, asking if there was anything they could do, to which she would receive a pleasant, solid no. Lawsuits are scary things; you don't want to draw attention to the personal in a professional setting. Months and months would pass. I imagine he would miss a class, and then another, and then blowing them off left and right, causing the department head to make him take a leave of absence. He wouldn't have the energy to say no. He definitely wouldn't have the energy to say help me. I imagine him deciding never to come back, leaving his wife and kids, and finally sleeping on the streets, too tired to walk to a new place, a new university, a new state, where he could be mad and homeless and anonymous.

But again, the university can't be that hard and ruthless an entity where someone would fail to say, Tell me what's going on with you.

No friend gave me help when I asked.

I like to believe that my alienation, self-imposed and otherwise, was deserved—my character defects are many. If it had been someone else, they would have been helped, I believe. I'm special, I like to think. I deserve what I got: nothing. I'm so unique that no one saw me as one of the many that are sick and waiting to die.

*

One time when I was at my worst, I went to a party thrown for a famous author. I stood in a room full of administrators. I was terrified. What happened if something inappropriate came out of my mouth? Being up for tenure, I was consistently afraid that I was going to offend. Or what if I started sobbing? What if a few of them had sympathy—they happened to have friends or family who were mentally ill and they would be willing to cut me a break? Give me more time to compile my materials.

What if they decided that not only did I need help, but also should be taken out of the classroom?

I shook everybody's hand, happily acting like myself to the best of my ability. One of the administrators I secretly disliked. I stared at him. Suddenly, a green wart appeared on his forehead, a witch's mark. There was part of me that wanted to touch it. The evil felt irresistible.

I resisted.

I like to think that the vision of the witch's wart was a result of my seeing the truth. I am a good judge of character; my intuitive powers are quite strong. Was the hallucination on some level a manifestation of what was metaphorically true?

*

Before *Mad Max: Fury Road* and badass Charlize Theron joined the series, you saw Mel Gibson as that apocalyptic hero racing around in a speeding car on a ruined earth.

Once my husband and I and a bunch of others were having a conversation about Mel. Everyone said he was an asshole, sexist, racist, homophobic, anti-Semitic, etc. His horrible tirades were made public; it was common knowledge.

Everyone said he should never be allowed to make another film. No one should forgive him.

"I bet he's mentally ill," I said later that night to my husband. "You need to allow for the possibility of forgiveness."

"You're gay," my husband said, "and you're letting that asshole off the hook. Let's say he was having a manic episode. He still didn't have to say those particular things."

"That's part of madness: You don't know what particular things will come to mind," I said.

"No," he said. "Madness is letting everyone off the hook for being an idiot."

*

A few years ago, I started telling my classes up front about my mental illness. I also tell them I'm gay, which isn't a big deal anymore as it was when I was an undergraduate. Sometimes though I get worried that they will connect the two in an unfortunate way and run back to their dorm room and tell their friends: "My teacher is mentally ill. And he's gay. He must be mentally ill because he's gay." But I don't think that turns out to be the case. And if it is, I've begun telling my classes explicitly that they have no direct relation on one another.

I don't know if I believe that. Maybe the two are linked. Maybe the American Psychiatric Association never should have declassified homosexuality as a mental disorder. They waited until 1973. There must be some truth to it if they waited so long.

Those are the sort of dumb thoughts I think when no one else is around.

Other times, I feel really powerful—and shall I dare say it?—brave. Which is exactly why I'm not. I know there's a lot of silent respect when I announce my illness. I'm not risking anything.

Teachers love an audience. I'm no different. Unfortunately, only so many students can fit in a classroom. The Quad was a huge space. You could have tons of students milling about, listening to you on and off. Perhaps Mad Max was wiser than me. He wasn't constrained by walls and a ceiling. When he looked up into the sky, he saw his words ascending toward the clouds. Maybe some of them made their way even farther.

*

Mental illness is talked about a lot more than it was in the '90s. I wonder if people would be more likely now to have aggressively stepped in, read the situation with Mad Max, and said, "This man is ill. He needs to see a doctor. Let's take this ill man to a doctor."

When I was mad, I was convinced that I was dying; the pain in my body would not relent. I took it upon myself to find out what was wrong.

I have a PhD. I was unwittingly trained to cure myself: to be saved through the act of reading books. That's what I did. I read every single book about pain I could find that matched my own. Everything became a self-help book. I felt I could find my sickness in a book. That's what an English professor does: He tries to attach words to name the actual thing. The problem was this: The actual thing was all words. Depression. Mania. Psychotic break.

My memory is weak, ruined. That's what mental illness and perhaps its necessary medications do to you.

Something must have made me realize what was wrong and then get help. I can't remember what it was. I can only remember that something from some godforsaken book pushed me onto a road of a recovery.

I'm an English professor who once never dared to rely on metaphors like "road to recovery." But I don't care anymore. I had a breakdown. I have a husband. I received my tenure. What more does the world want from me?

I've earned my metaphors. I've earned my sanity.

*

When I struggle to keep myself from suicidal thoughts, I think of Mad Max. I picture him preaching, working those long hours, hours longer than any professor's, determined to teach the world what he's learned. Perhaps his decision never to get help was an act of kindness. Nothing could stop him from begging us to save ourselves. Of course, at my worst, I am even more thankful and full of soulless empathy. I understand Mad Max and all I have to say is one thing: Thank God that's not me. That is what empathy is, after all: rejoicing that you're not suffering as someone else is. Mad Max taught me to live outside of myself, to hold on to my words, to take a deep breath in between my thoughts, and not think as much as I would like, as much as I believe I once needed to survive.

Inspiration

No movie biography has disturbed me more than Ed Harris's *Pollock*. My dislike for the movie centers around one key scene: the moment Jackson Pollock finds his Inspiration. It's the scene that attempts to show Pollock's discovery of his Action paintings. The Big Moment of Discovery.

This is the Moment: Pollock is doing one of his more typical paintings. He drops his brush. Paint splatters all over the floor. Frustrated, he takes a step back. He recognizes Genius. This is the beginning of his Abstract Expressionism.

Could there be anything more reductive than representing Pollock's Inspiration as the accidental dropping of a paintbrush?

I confess that I avoided seeing the movie when it first came to theatres, even after Marcia Gay Harden won the Best Supporting Actress Oscar for playing the role of Harris's sassy, long-suffering wife. Movie biographies bother me. They try to cover way too much time, advancing to the Major Dramatic Scenes with shameful excitement. They're also often dull and earnest.

Before I saw *Pollock*, I read numerous interviews with Ed Harris about his process in making the film. (Should we assume that Harris tripped over a copy of a Pollock biography, causing him to hit his head, motivating the epiphany that the book should be made into a movie starring himself?) I heard about all the typical setbacks. The years it took to attract investors. The painstaking research. The usual production problems. It sounded like good news copy. Only an unkind person like myself could fail to be touched.

I can still remember the fateful night several other English teachers and I ended up in Blockbuster Video, desperately trying to find a movie to rent. It was the first time we all went out together and everyone wanted to look respectable.

"Has anyone seen the latest Stephen Segal movie?" I said.

"Who's he?" someone said.

"I don't know," I lied. "The cover looked interesting." I put the movie back on the shelf and decided that I wouldn't offer any recommendations.

"How about *Pollock?*" someone else said.

Everyone agreed and we walked out of the video store, victorious.

When it came to the Moment of Inspiration, I burst into laughter. Someone thought I was choking on popcorn, so they grabbed the remote control and asked me if I was OK.

"I was laughing," I said.

"At what?"

"That scene," I said. "It's ridiculous. To think that the birth of Abstract Expressionism is predicated on Pollock's accidental dropping of a paintbrush is insane."

Everyone looked at me like I was crazy.

"Do you think you're being fair?" someone else said.

"Fair?"

"Yes, fair," the person said. "Inspiration is a very difficult thing to represent on film."

I couldn't disagree with my colleague. Inspiration is a very difficult thing to represent on film. Or for that matter explain in any way. But I couldn't drop the subject. I pushed it further: "Hubris."

"Hubris," someone repeated.

"Hubris," I said. "That's what this movie is guilty of. That's the sin I attach to Ed Harris. He's an artist. A really good actor. How dare he think that he can explain a fellow artist's inspiration in one quick, glib scene."

Someone excused himself to go to the bathroom. Someone else went to get more popcorn. Two others marched outside and shared a cigarette. There was one other person in the room. He was in the philosophy department and he never engaged in conversation. He hoarded all his thoughts. His name was Phil.

"So," Phil said. "What else do you think of the movie?"

"I didn't know much about Jackson Pollock going into the movie," I said. "And having watched the movie for about an hour now, I don't think I know anything much more."

He looked at me with the blankest of expressions. This made me want to rant more. But I had nothing else to say. I was tired.

"So," he said, "the movie hasn't offered you any insight into the character of Jackson Pollock?" He spoke slowly and deliberately. I could imagine him paraphrasing his students' comments in class, and his students cringing, wondering how their words were inevitably going to make them look stupid.

"Yes," I said.

"Is that a good thing or a bad thing?"

"When I see a biography, I want to know something new about the person. Isn't that why we rented this film?"

"Is it?" Phil said. "Or is it an odd success of the film that Ed Harris chooses not to offer any dazzling new psychological insights into Jackson Pollock? Harris allows the superficial myths surrounding Pollock to remain untouched, unexamined. Like the domestic fighting. Like the drinking. Like the depression. His refusal to interrogate is an act of kindness. Harris doesn't pursue what makes Pollock tick, because he knows he can't do it. And to pretend to do so is ultimately unethical. So he uses the myths as a way of showing off his own acting talents. While leaving the human mysteries behind those very myths alone."

"But what about the scene I was talking about? The moment of his Inspiration?"

"Comedy," Phil said. "Pure comedy."

At the time I didn't know what to say, so I said nothing except the obvious: "Inspiration is a funny thing." It's not like I could offer any effective solutions to Harris's dilemma: representing Inspiration in a convincing, edifying way. You couldn't show Pollock summoning the Devil, engaging in some sort of Faustian bargain, offering his full mortality for Artistic Genius. Nor could you ask Julia Roberts to contribute a cameo as a Muse, offering sassy, cogent advice whenever Harris's Pollock grows tired, inert.

All I knew was I wanted Something More.

"Don't we all?" Phil said.

"Is that bad?" I said.

"No," Phil said. "But you're forgetting something."

"What?"

"There are the paintings," he said. "There are always the paintings."

On Fragmentation

Once I developed a severe case of uticaria. I can still remember the ER nurse surveying the red splotches all over my skin. I asked her if I should be worried. "You're still breathing. That's always a good thing," she said. That's when I knew I was in trouble.

What was weird about these hives was that they would move. You'd see a rash on my upper neck; if you closed your eyes for a second, they'd disappear and show up somewhere else: my shoulder, arm, or even forehead. They wouldn't stop moving.

You couldn't trace a definite trajectory—the appearance of the hives seemed almost arbitrary. After I accepted the fact that this uticaria was going to continue indefinitely, my relation to Time became different. I couldn't pinpoint the moment when something revealed itself and then when it vanished. Everything was blurry and fragmented.

*

I never trust people who love Sappho. It seems cowardly. It's always easy to say that you like something based on a few fragments. Or maybe I'm the coward. I always want to fill in the blanks with unambiguous solutions. I always believe that if you look hard enough, you can find something else that you see as definite, essential.

*

Years ago, I had a nervous breakdown, culminating in a diagnosis of bipolar disorder. What bothered me most was sleeplessness. Before I received the proper diagnosis, it turned out I was wrongly prescribed an antidepressant, jettisoning me into mania.

I didn't fall asleep for three days. I lost track of time. Wakefulness never seemed to end. I needed to experience time in smaller stretches. Little fragments of eternity.

*

When I grade freshman composition essays, I sense that I always become more annoyed when I spot a sentence fragment as opposed to a run-on sentence. How American is it to assume that more is more?

*

When I was manic, I couldn't sit down. I didn't know what got into me. I didn't know how I was going to continue at the rate I was going. I thought I was going to die.

I decided that if I was going to die I had to write my mother a love letter.

The best way I knew how to write someone a love letter was to write a book.

How to begin?

I sat down at the computer and typed a single quotation my mother had once said to me.

I had been excessively apologizing to people for things I didn't have any control over.

She slapped me and said: "Don't live your life like a woman. Don't live your life as an apology."

I read my mother the quotation. "I said that?" she said. "That's pretty damn good."

"That's part of a new book I'm writing," I said. "It's the first sentence."

"Whatever happened to Once Upon a Time?"

*

It seems that more and more people are structuring their essays into piecemeal sections. Little bits. Sometimes enumerated, sometimes not. Sometimes titled, sometimes not. When you ask them why they structured the essay the way that they did, they'll say something like, "I want the reader to draw their own conclusions." Which always sounds like a cop-out. Isn't that why you became a writer in the first place? To draw someone else's conclusions for them in an artful, honest way?

*

During the course of writing my memoir, I showed my mother my fragmented notes, all from childhood.

We made a pact. She would write one of three things next to my scribbling. I told her to tear up the sheets of paper and place each fragment in one of three piles: one marked "OK," one marked "You're making things up," one marked, "Too personal." Without asking for explanation, I gave her back the ones she labeled "Too personal." "You can burn those if you want," I said. For the ones marked "You're making things up," we talked about them, trying to reach a compromise. We always did.

I took the fragments marked "OK" and "You're making things up" and turned them into full-length scenes. It oddly didn't take much time to add transition, descriptions of place, elaborating on characters and conversations. Before I knew it, all those fragments that were in the end finally agreed on by both of us as the "acceptable raw material" for my book were transformed. My fragments had become whole.

I sent them to my mother for approval.

She brought them all back to me in a big disorganized pile. Now they all had the same comment: "You're making things up."

Then she handed me back the stack of sheets she'd marked "Too personal." She hadn't thrown them away. "Use these," she said.

*

One of my creative writing teachers once said to me the digressions in a piece of writing are almost always the most interesting parts. If you create an essay-in-fragments, you never really have time to digress. You're always looking for the end. You have no time to go anywhere other than forward. Detours aren't acceptable.

*

What is complexity but a lot of simple things strung together?

*

Does illness always preclude form? Does illness always preclude the fact that memories needed to be forgotten? Is trying to create a coherent narrative a sickness in and of itself?

*

A memoir-in-fragments invites non sequiturs. Accepting a life as a series of non sequiturs may be the most honest way not only of writing but also of living.

*

A fragment is in itself incomplete. The conundrum: No matter how many fragments you assemble you can never create the actual thing.

*

A memoir-in-fragments always encourages me not to read it from beginning to end. Once I told a friend that.

"That's not cool," she said.

"What isn't?"

"You read it from beginning to end. That's the way the author intended it. If he meant for you to read the thirty-fifth fragment, then he would have put that first. The first is always the first. I hope you feel bad about what you've been doing."

"Now I do," I said.

"Good."

*

A creative writing teacher about essays-in-fragments: "If you write the perfect fragment, you won't need the rest of the essay. All you'll need is the fragment."

*

I hate jigsaw puzzles. So many little tiny pieces. So many fragments hopeful to find themselves in a completed puzzle. Once a potential boyfriend told me, "I hate jigsaw puzzles. Why would you want to create an image someone else has already created?"

That's when I knew I was in love.

*

Ever since my nervous breakdown, I've lost some of my short-term memory. My husband and I will be watching a TV show, and five minutes after a pivotal scene occurs, I'll have to ask for clarification as to what happened. Our nights usually consist of him stopping the DVR, rewinding, offering a synopsis, and then replaying. I'm not just talking about shows everyone sees as intricate and complicated, like *The Wire* or *Game of Thrones*. I'm even talking about *Gossip Girl*. He's a patient man so he doesn't get too angry. He even sort of enjoys it.

Our viewing is so fragmented that it can take three hours to finish one show. Which isn't a bad thing. Now finding our way from the beginning through the end feels like more than an experience. It feels like a feat. Like we accomplished something big.

This has made us grow even closer.

*

A memoir-in-fragments confesses the disposability of literature. Let's face it: There's always something you can cut out
that no one will notice. And if they do notice, they'll just
assume it's in the white space, begging for their attention.

*

When I first started sending my mother fragments, she said,
"What are you going to do with all these things?"

"I don't know," I said. "Maybe I'll keep them the way they
are."

She said, "That's crazy. Everyone will think you've written
a book of poetry."

"Maybe I have," I said.

"Oh no!" she said. "No one reads poetry. How am I supposed to become famous? Respect your mother. Turn me
into prose. You owe me that."

*

When you're writing an essay-in-fragments, should each
fragment be a complete thing in and of itself? Or does
it need to transcend itself, existing for something larger?
Should we even think of transcendence as a goal in literature? Should the goal simply be to allow?

*

I wrote an essay-in-fragments for a creative writing teacher.
During the workshop, he said: *Kill all your darlings.*

I raised my hand and asked, "Can you be a little more
specific? They're all my darlings."

My mother is suffering
from uterine cancer and all
I can think about is the '80s.

My mother is suffering from uterine cancer
and all I can think about is the '80s   .
when my gay friends died of AIDS

and I ditched their funerals,
pretending I had a cold
and didn't want to get anyone else sick,

especially those with weakened immune systems,
because then more people would die
and there would be more funerals

and our calendars were already filled with remembrances
of friends' uninspired suicides and upcoming estate sales,
which never brought me any goodies

except a pink flamingo lawn ornament
that I gave to my mother after explaining
that it had a high "kitsch" value,

to which she replied, "If it has worth, then you keep it,"
to which I replied, "You put that pink bird
on a gay man's lawn,

all it becomes is camp."
The other day I read some lines of a poem
by a popular young gay poet

and he criticized the AIDS quilt
and I wanted to search for his address
and send him hate mail,

telling him that he will be punished
for his lack of generational respect.
In the same magazine, he wrote a poem about PrEP,

and I don't know
if it was good or bad writing, only
that I wondered if any of my friends are still

alive and taking the drug themselves.
Like Marcus who whenever he had sex put a smiley face
on the designated day of his kitchen calendar.

Once I noticed that there were four smiley faces
on May 4, Labor Day, and I wanted to say,
"You definitely must have been working hard,"

but I didn't: the fantasy of him screwing men while I ate
overcooked barbeque at my mother's house
proved momentarily entertaining. I told him

to be careful out there, and he spit
on my shoes, and said, "We're all going to die.
I want to go out doing what I love."

I don't dream of my dead friends, not
because I'm afraid that I'm going to be overwhelmed
by sadness, but I never liked them. They were shiny

and dumb. Why am I so judgmental of those
who didn't go to college? Why am I thinking
such things when my mother is sick in a hospital bed,

bored with crossword puzzles, hoping
that if she succeeds in conquering them,
she'll be able to convince herself her mind is intact

and then be more able to make a decision about chemo?
My mother never graduated high school;
however, I found her lack charming,

but with my friends, it was disgraceful.
When I went to college, they promised
that when I visited for the summer,

they would lavish Gap's Friends & Family Discounts
on me, which I would never cash in on,
because dressing poorly was proof

that I was better than them.
I was too busy searching for knowledge
while they were looking for that pec-hugging

sweater or ass-caressing pants that made them
more than fuckable. Once my mother asked,
"Why aren't you more like them?" I didn't know

how to translate her question so I simply said,
"Because I don't want to be like you." Her response:
"Makes sense." Now, the nurses have used restraints

after my mother tore her IVs from her wrist
and I wonder what she would say if I mocked her gown,
her bland, disposable single article of clothing. So I do.

I say, "You look good," which gets no response
except from the male nurse who smiles and says,
"Your mother is not an easy patient,"

and then puts on a pair of plastic gloves
and readies the needle, and I say, "Why
are you wearing those on your hands? Do you think

my mother is unclean?" and I can't stop myself,
so I continue: "She is not a dirty woman,"
and, of course, that's not enough either, and I add,

"You made her soil her bed. When are you going
to clean it up?" He puts the needle down and raises
his hands in the air and says, "I give up,"

making me think of one of the few times I went
to visit a sick friend with AIDS: I stood outside
of the hospital room and saw the ventilator

move up and down, and said, "I can't go in. What if
I disturb the harmony with my footsteps?,"
and the nurse said, "Don't be silly. Just put these on,"

and gave me a pair of plastic gloves, and I said,
"Another," and he said, "You only need one pair,"
and I said, "Another pair to put over these,"

and he said, "So you're the coward your friends
talk about," and I said, "You can't be too careful,"
and he said, "Yes. Actually you can."

Everyone is despicable for at least one reason.
Like my own undergraduate students who don't
know how to rhyme their poems.

They'll never become familiar with gay poet
Thom Gunn who everybody once loved for being the first
to write about AIDS in classical forms.

From one of his back covers, you can tell
he's quite attractive and I'm sure
everyone wanted to fuck him

as they would now, and I don't know how he escaped
without contracting HIV
(he died of a banal heart attack!). I know, I know,

we shouldn't assume the narrator of the poem
is the author himself.
That's the kind of man I am:

I don't believe in any lyric "I."
I don't have time for any mind games.
The "I" is either you or the poem's a fraud.

Does the fact that my mother adopted me make me a
        sham?
Am I as entitled to grief as my father is
even though he ditched her for a woman

who looked exactly like her
which caused her to exclaim,
"You could have found plenty of upgrades,

why settle for what you already have?"
and then said to me, "That's why I adopted you.
I knew I'd get a son that was better

than one I could produce," and rather than seeing
that as an expression of love, which it was,
I wondered if even back then

my mother knew something someday
was going to happen to her uterus,
and didn't want to risk

that cancer would happen then, to me, by extension.
Did she save my life before I was even born?
Now, my mother shakes from being cold in her hospital bed

and I imagine cutting off a piece of the AIDS quilt
for my mother and draping it across her body,
and then if she still was shivering, I would cut another piece

and another and another,
the whole time transforming the pieces of the quilt
into something wholly ridiculous,

a cross-stitched hazmat suit. The last time
I thought of contamination was 1983
when I had to call an ambulance for my friend who had
        AIDS

and the audacity to slit his wrists in his bathtub
after we had spent the entire night
watching reruns of *The Golden Girls,*

which I never liked, even though it's blasphemy
to be gay and to talk ill of Bea Arthur
whose cheeks I wanted to pinch

until she begged me for mercy
which I would give as long as she agreed
to commit to an emotion other than

embitterment. Two men arrived at the house
and they were both wearing hazmat suits.
My suicidal friend's apartment was in the gay

neighborhood and they must have received
a number of phone calls from the dying.
I walked up to one of them and poked at his hazmat suit,

because I always wanted to know what one felt like,
and it was worth the indiscretion.
I received what I needed right then and there:

the chance to touch death.
One of the men unzipped his arm coverings
and touched my shoulder

(the closest thing to good sex I've ever had!).
He said, "You are going to live. Don't worry."
My response: "Oh."

If I were a real poet, I would be exclaiming O!
A big fat O. A big fat O Mother.
O my big fat motherfucking Mother,

don't begin to moan because
all I think is, "You did this to yourself,
you should have had a hysterectomy,"

which is so gross to feel toward any mother,
or any woman,
especially your own, but I do,

and to stifle my anger, I imagine cutting
that same AIDS quilt
into handkerchief-sized pieces, and shoving

them into the mouth of the nurse, and then yes,
O yes, and then into my own.
Until he and I can't breathe and we beg for mercy

that no one can give,
not even an indifferent God.
I wonder if my mother's hospital bed

was ever occupied
by someone who had AIDS,
and I even say that to my mother who replies,

"Which do you think is a more painful death:
AIDS or uterine cancer?"
and I say, "It's a toss-up,"

but my mother isn't satisfied with that answer,
so she presses the emergency button
for the nurse who looks bored

with my mother's faux urgent pleas,
but answers her question nonetheless: ALS.
I want to crawl into my mother's womb and hide

from a world that has nothing better to do
than kill men dressed in clothes finer
than any words

some embarrassingly overeducated poet could utter.
Once I ran into a friend of a friend of a friend
who died of AIDS. At first, he didn't

recognize me, and then did a double-take,
and said that he heard a story about me way back when:
one of my friends had been diagnosed with HIV,

and he was taking the news quite well,
talking about his medication
and the teams of doctors he had organized,

and I said to him, "Why am I not happier than you?
I'm not the one who's going to die."
Once my mother accompanied me to the funeral

of a neighbor's son who died in a gruesome way
from AIDS, and after the wake,
my friends and I stood in a corner and gossiped

about how many men he had slept with.
It took them a moment to admit they had sex with him,
and my mother flashed me a disappointed look

that said Why-didn't-you?
It was one of those horrible moments
when all you can say is the truth:

"I'm sorry." And I'm sorry for not knowing what a uterus is,
no matter how ridiculous that may seem,
as it provokes my mother to say,

"Are you stupid?" which causes both of us to laugh,
and I don't know if I should be offended or happy
that my mother has accepted my gayness

so completely that she accepts I'm indifferent
to the female anatomy,
which, of course, I am. Or was.

"It's inside," I say, and she says, "Pretty good guess,"
and then she says, "Don't ever feel bad
for not being a slut. It just wasn't your thing.

You're not ugly.
Some of your friends were just beautiful."
I want to tell you this poem would have been better

if it wasn't for AIDS,
but that would be a lie.
If I wasn't avoiding funerals, I would have found

something else to do. Like volleyball. Like calligraphy.
Like arts and crafts. Once I did visit a friend
in a psychiatric ward who was suffering

from AIDS-related dementia,
which might have been a pleasant reprieve
from all the physical pain,

and he was so happy that I visited
he made me a ceramic blue piggy bank.
It sat on my bedside table, the one my mother found

at an estate sale of an unremarkable community leader
who died of AIDS.
A day after my mother's cancer diagnosis,

she came into my room and saw the pig
and she snorted, claiming it was odd
that I would exhibit my own grade-school creations.

But then she said, "It's a small miracle.
I hope I told you that when you were a kid."
I didn't say it wasn't mine. I offered it to her.

Of course, she took it.

She put it on the mantel above the fireplace.

"Dump my ashes in it," she said. "I'll be your pig."

V

On Marxism,
My Mother's Body, and the
State of Creative Nonfiction

I wrote a memoir about my mother no one read. It won a contest no one entered. Except for ten people including myself. The memoir was published. The editors were nice people who needed a tax write-off. There was a small cash prize. There were royalties, but since no one purchased it, I didn't make any money that way.

However, at the time, I was an assistant professor at a small, rural liberal arts college in western New York. The memoir solidified my chances of tenure: The book was mentioned consistently in the chain of recommendation letters from the head of the department to the president. I was promoted with tenure. You could say that I made $50,000 a year (my salary) from a book no one read.

My own mother didn't read the finished book. She might not even have looked at the cover.

*

Revenge is never a solution. I know this. But it never stops me from trying. The striving to destroy someone feels good. If I convince myself it won't have a positive result, I assume it's because I'm too much of a coward (or lazy).

When I first started writing about my mother, I had to ask, "Am I doing this out of some sort of revenge?"

It wasn't a mean book. But it did deal with her shoplifting, her disappointment with marriage, her taking me out of school just so we could go to the movies etc. etc.

Any decent person asks why one reveals personal information. Once a teacher told me: "It doesn't matter how they appear. On the page, you're God. And you've got to decide how things go down."

Another one said: "We always end up writing about people who have caused us problems. If they don't like what you wrote, they should have behaved."

There's also all those other boring creative nonfiction debates that we talk about: What is a fact? Are sometimes metaphors more "accurate" than the truth? Is there an ethical issue in having direct quotations in a memoir? After all, you haven't tape-recorded the conversations. Etc. Etc. Etc.

I'm a simple person. My litmus test: If you feel like a complete asshole after you're done writing, throw the thing away. Your heart knows the truth.

*

My mother is dying.

She is dying of uterine cancer and dementia and the aftereffects of a stroke. Part by part, her body and mind are dying. When people ask me what's wrong with her, I usually choose to tell them about one of her afflictions. "Cancer," I'll say to one colleague. And then to a different colleague, I'll say: "Alzheimer's." Sometimes I get worried that people will exchange stories and think I'm lying.

This has extended into my writing. I fear editors will think I'm piling on the illnesses to get sympathy, publication.

At the same time, I don't give a shit. It's the truth.

*

Even before my book, I wrote about my mother. My mother is my currency. People love stuff about gay men and their mothers. When I first applied to MFA programs, I turned in a portfolio that dealt with my mother. I was accepted and received a TA-ship. Later I applied to get my PhD. Again, the work was about my mother. I received a substantial fellowship. You could say my mother was supporting me all those years even though she never gave me a dime.

"Graduate school?" she said. "How can you still be in school if you graduated?"

She never graduated high school. Until her breakdown, she worked three menial jobs to keep us afloat.

You could say I choose graduate school because I didn't want to be like her. I didn't want to ever work for a living.

*

I don't use metaphors when I write. No similes. I don't allow my students to either. I forbid them. One semester I threatened to lower their semester grade if they did.

Is this a stupid thing to do?

Yes, of course it is.

But I get scared of them. My mother will not be here much longer, I fear. Who has time for the "lyric" essay when the end is near? You need to write as simply and as plainly as possible. Everything has to be free of any flourish, any hidden gesture. No add-ons. No substitutions. As plain and as exact as a dollar bill.

*

My memoir doesn't include most of the important facts about my mother. Even in the section called "The Important Facts about My Mother." Here are some that I left out: She has undiagnosed bipolar disorder; she could be mean and violent; she was a foster child who was abused on a regular basis.

I never thought about putting them in the memoir. They seemed unimportant, I guess. I didn't want to pathologize her. Plus some things are personal. They shouldn't be written for everyone to read. Now after all these years later, I can say that if I wrote a memoir, those are things that I would include. Those are the things everyone writes about. Those are the things that could possibly make money. Those are things that could make my writing be read by more than a dozen people (if that isn't a gross inflation).

But would it be more honest? And is honesty even the issue here?

I don't think so. Maybe less. I wrote a comedy. The naming of things would make it a drama.

Both cost you something: one dignity, the other legitimacy. I don't know which impacts which.

*

My mother threw me out of the house when I was a teenager. It wasn't because I'm gay. It was because my father divorced her, paid little in child support, and she couldn't support two kids. I was the older. I was the one who should leave. It sounded reasonable.

I am now in my mid-forties. I saw her two times during a twenty-six-year gap. I always convinced myself that I was too busy to make amends. I didn't want to intrude; I was scared. She and my brother live together. She lost everything and was homeless, unable to keep a job due to her unpredictable mood swings. My brother took her in.

Once I applied for a $3,000 travel scholarship when I was a PhD student. I wrote a nonfiction proposal claiming I was going to do archival work in England about Joice Heth, who was one of P. T. Barnum's first acts. She claimed to be the 165-year-old mammy of General George Washington.

It was a lie. I never had any plans of going to England. I was going to use the money for an extended trip to see my mother. I'd take her out on the town. Every night. I'd fix everything.

I won the fellowship. I used the money to pay for dental surgery and a new state-of-the-art TV. I sent my mom a $50 check.

*

As I type this essay, I see the paragraphs and I think of each one as a body bag, each holding a part of my mother, each rolling down the page with an unaggressive deliberateness.

*

I wrote the bulk of my memoir when I was near having to go on the job market for a tenure-track job. My focus was on poetry. But there was no way you could get a job without a book. Or even two. I know it's even worse now.

Nonfiction writers could still get tenure-track jobs without books, though. I knew you had to have published something in the genre. So: I wrote fragments that I thought might turn into a full-length memoir. Not that it mattered. The pieces were one paragraph to seven pages long. I had dozens of them. I sent three or four fragments to a variety of magazines at a time, always simultaneously submitting. They got picked up often. I've never had more acceptances from editors.

And that's how I got my job. I could put on my resume that I published all these "essays." People don't have time to read all your work. They didn't know an essay was often just a page in length, if that. A number were less. All they saw was the sheer quantity that appeared on the resume. I looked like a prolific practitioner of the craft.

I was offered the job. The best prize: primo health insurance.

*

I'm a very privileged person. Even though I am still paying off the $100,000 I took out in loans during my school years.

Now I am a full professor. I don't need to publish with the same productivity as I did before. I'm OK. I even have a cute, bald husband who edits my stuff with a kindness he showed me before we were even officially married. We've been together for twenty-plus years. As long as I publish something every two years, I am pretty much safe. At least for now.

So: It's a perfect time for my mother to be dying. I'm on sabbatical and I have enough money for occasional brief visits.

Still, the future is scary for gay men. No kids, estranged family. Who is going to take care of us when we get old? I won't be inheriting anything as my mother collects $600 in social security. What will happen to us when we are solely dependent on the kindness of strangers and a paltry annuity?

*

It's tough to write about my mother since she got sick. I can barely do it. It hurts too much. The only reason I can write this essay is that I'm writing about her alongside other issues: the professionalization of creative writing, an implicit Marxist bent, my career. I slip her in when I feel strong, when I feel it's time, when this essay needs to appear to have heart.

*

I am not an attractive man. This is not an attempt at self-deprecation. It is a fact.

My mother isn't a looker either.

Her illnesses have made her truly decrepit.

I was so repulsed that I took a picture of her and sent it to a friend. She didn't say anything. She didn't say she didn't look too bad. My friend pitied me.

That's why I won't describe my mother's body in an essay. I like someone to see the actual picture of her. I like to see their disgust. It makes me feel like I've accomplished something. I'm not sure what. But for a few moments, I feel completed in a way that writing an essay has never made me feel.

*

In a recent issue of *Creative Nonfiction,* the celebrated essayist (and friend of mine) Nicole Walker writes about something she names as "the braided essay." It seems to me the braided essay consists of essentially two strands: one strand which is straight-up memoir, the other one based on empirical evidence, fact, research, history. Both often rely on fragments. Think Terry Tempest Williams's *Refuge.* In that book, Williams shifts between two different narratives: one about her mother dying of breast cancer (memoir), the other about the destruction of environment (fact-based research). The twinning compliments, supplements, deflates, inflates, highlights, obscures. As Walker says: "What is creative nonfiction writing but the shaping and reshaping of self against fact?"

I want to say to her: *Everything.*

I want to write about my mother. I don't care about anything else. She is dying. My mother needs a miracle, not research.

I'm afraid that I see the braided essay as fraudulent. Is it a response to the anxiety one feels in writing about oneself? As if by focusing on yourself and only yourself, you're doing something that is automatically selfish? So: I need to justify that choice by also showing myself as invested in the Great Political Issues of our times? I find that most people who practice the braided essay are almost always greatly invested in science—they can intersperse more or less random facts to give their writing gravitas. (Of course, there are exceptions. Like Williams. Like Walker.)

In other words, is there cowardice embedded in the braided essay? Are those who dedicate themselves to the braided essay secretly wanting to write no-holds-barred memoirs but scared of being seen as navel-gazers?

I will write about my mother until I die. I have no apologies. No Emily Dickinson here. I don't want to tell it slant. I'm all about going forward.

Deleted Scenes from My Unpublished Memoir

I never wanted to be a gay man. I wanted to be a lisp. I wanted to be something that came out of someone's mouth wrong. I wanted the sound of my body to be disturbed. I don't believe in euphony. I have faith in the beauty of the stutter and the slur. That's how I came to realize myself as queer: I listened to someone else's voice and asked if they were talking to me. Yes or no didn't matter. All that mattered: the pause.

Once a man whispered something into my ear. I looked confused. "Did you hear that?" he asked.

"No," I said. "I can never make out the words of a future lover."

*

I was obsessed with dolls. In sixth grade, I wanted a Cabbage Patch Kid. My mother took me everywhere to find one. We had no luck. It was Christmastime. She kept on calling store after store, hoping that some place would have just received a shipment.

That's what ended up happening. We rushed to a Sears in another city. The saleswoman met us at the door. "We have dozens and dozens of Cabbage Patch Kids," she said. "It's too bad that no one wants them."

We couldn't believe it. We followed her to the aisle. There were rows and rows of them. They were all black. The saleswoman apologized. "The white ones are all gone," she said. "They sell out quick."

I took one off the shelf. His birth certificate read: Reggie Jackson. My mother bought him for me.

*

My brother always ordered the same thing for breakfast. "French toast and bacon. Crisp on the bacon." I loved that he felt the need to use the word *crisp*. It was unnecessary. Or perhaps it wasn't. His bacon always turned out crisp. He single-handedly taught me the power of words.

*

My first crush was on a Japanese exchange student. His name was Koichi. It was eighth grade. I hadn't even figured out that I was gay. When he moved away, I was bereft. I wrote him a letter a week, sometimes more. After a few months, he asked me to stop writing. He wrote: "There is no such thing as a special parting. Yet every parting is special." I don't know if he cribbed that from a famous book.

*

Once I picked up a guy at a bar who had been released from prison. I invited him back to my apartment. I liked that I was hanging out with a convict. It made me feel edgy.

Once we got to my place, he said, "I'm tired. Tomorrow is my first day of work." He showed me his pair of work gloves. I was impressed. He set them down on my desk. During the night, I wanted him gone. I'm not sure why. I didn't know what to do. This is what I decided: I set my alarm clock four hours ahead of the actual time. He woke up and he saw the clock and put on his clothes and ran out the door. He thought he was late.

Twenty minutes later, he came back and knocked, yelling, "Why did you do that to me?" I didn't say anything. He said he knew I was there. Eventually a neighbor said she was calling the police. I could hear him leaning up against the door, crying. "Can you at least give me my work gloves back? I left them on the desk," he said. "It's my first day of work since I got out of jail. Please. I need to show up with my work gloves. I need to be able to do the job. They told us not to forget them. They won't give us a second pair."

I didn't open the door. I made myself believe I was scared for my life. He had been in prison after all. I went back to bed. This is the worst thing I've ever done. This is my greatest sin.

*

I remember my father's chessboards—at least a dozen full-size ones!—spread out all over the living room. I never saw him play chess with someone in person. We had so few friends. However, he did play games with people through the mail, shooting back and forth moves on postcards. He had little magnetic chessboards with little magnetic pieces. I felt he treasured those the most. Whenever he received a move in the mail, he marched over to one of the boards, picked up the designated piece and made the change. Once my father and I fought. I swore revenge. When he was not home, I rearranged his pieces on his chessboards, making a whole new game. He never noticed. I can still remember when he got a card in the mail from one of the competitors who wrote: "It seems like you don't care about this game. You're sending me moves that make no sense." It was the only time I've ever seen my father cry.

*

My senior-year English teacher was shuttled throughout the district schools. He was always accused of inappropriate behavior toward male students. He never paid attention to me. He asked the class to submit poems for a contest sponsored by the National Council of Teachers of English. I knew how to win awards. I wrote a poem called "My Bearded English Teacher." It compared my teacher to Fred Astaire, his podium to Ginger Rogers. I wrote that they waltzed around the room, employing an extended metaphor. English teachers eat that stuff up. He loved it. The National Council loved it. I won first prize. Before the school officially announced the award, he took me after class and told me the good news. I went to hug him. He hugged me back. I went to hug him again and he took a step back. A month later he was fired for molesting my best friend.

*

One time when I was in graduate school, a dozen of us were playing Truth or Dare. I always chose the dares. I liked the possibility of kissing someone. Even if they were unattractive. Once a friend dared me to dance. He knew that nothing terrified me more than that. If I went to a bar with music, I'd pretend I hurt my leg.

"There's one catch," my friend said. "We're all going to have our eyes shut while you do it." I danced. I looked at everybody as I did. They all had their eyes shut. It was so quiet. All you could hear was the sound of my shoes against the floor. That was the cruelest thing anyone has ever done to me.

*

One year for my husband's birthday, I did not plan anything. We ended up taking the uninspired route: fancy restaurant and then a movie. There wasn't much of a choice when it came to the films. One was called *Away from Her*. It was about Alzheimer's disease.

My husband's aunt was dealing with dementia. I knew the movie was going to be up for an Academy Award. One of my traditions: seeing every movie that is up for an Oscar. "I'll go with you sometime to see it," he said. "I just don't want to watch that on my birthday."

I was afraid it was going to leave the theatres before I got to see it. I begged him. I said: "The movie might make you feel good, especially on your birthday. It's healthy to weep every so often. And when better to indulge?"

We saw the movie. He cried during the last half. Afterward, I said, "Didn't that make you feel better about life?"

He said, "She died."

"Exactly," I said. "And you're alive."

*

One time the building where I teach was being renovated because of the finding of asbestos. I never understood how there could be men in hazmat suits wandering around while students were moving from class to class. I remember sitting in my classroom teaching and seeing particles of something descend from the ceiling to the floor. They floated closer and closer to me. If I hadn't seen them, would these little dots of death have entered my body and sent me toward my end? Was it wrong to be relieved that you could die from something so small, something you might have easily not noticed?

*

I was always told not to look at the eclipse. You'll burn out the corneas in your eyes. I couldn't help it. I didn't want to hide my eyes from something so grand. So: I looked. One of my grade-school classmates saw me. She called for the teacher, who ran toward me and tackled me. I kept on looking. I told everyone what I saw. They all gathered around me and listened. After I told them, they clapped—without any cue from the teacher. It is the only time in my life I ever felt like a hero.

*

After I left my parents' house to go to college and until I turned thirty-three, I never slept in a bed. They scared me. I moved into an apartment with my husband. "It's time you slept in a bed," he said. "With me."

*

At carnivals I played the duck game in which there's a conveyer belt with bright yellow ducks ready to be plucked. You grab one and whatever picture is on the bottom is your prize. Once nothing was there. It was impossible. The sign even said, "Everyone wins." My mother complained. The circus operator said, "Sometimes a duck is useless."

*

I remember my first graduate creative writing workshop. We were all required to bring a family photo that mattered to us. The pictures circulated around the table. There was a photo of a young girl leaning against a tree. A man was staring at her. I didn't know whose picture it was. I held it up and said, "This man doesn't want the picture to be taken. Now there is proof."

The teacher said it was her picture. She said, "You understand." And then put the picture in her purse.

*

Every kid has the sex talk. My father called me into the bathroom. He was shaving. He turned to me and said, "Do you know what tits are?"

*

In high school, I wanted to be a star in the theatre department. They never gave me roles. I dreamed of playing the character of Lenny in *Of Mice and Men*. (Lenny suffered brain damage as a kid.) I practiced my lines. I worked for months. I'd force my friends to act out scenes with me. "Do you think I play someone with brain damage well?" I said. They never wanted to give me a straight answer.

"To be successful," one of them said to me, "you have to have a certain look in your eyes." They told me I didn't have that special look yet. For hours and hours, I stared in the mirror and tried to see a reflection of a soul that suffered.

*

My favorite TV game show was *Press Your Luck*. You had to collect spins through answering trivia questions to make your way around an eighteen-space game board. This was the best part of the show: the Whammy. It was a red, plump cartoon creature wearing a cape. If you landed on any of the spaces that featured the Whammy, everything you amassed was taken away from you. A little cartoon would flash on the screen showing the Whammy chased, blown up, skewered, or facing an endless series of humiliations and/or deaths. I always wanted the Whammy to win. Only now do I realize the story of the Whammy is as powerful as any old medieval morality play.

*

In grade school, an unfamiliar woman told my friends and me to get in her car. She was a substitute for someone else in the carpool. All my friends knew who she was. I didn't. I refused to get in. Every kid is told you're not supposed to get in cars with strangers. There was a blizzard going on. "You're going to freeze to death," the woman said.

I ran. I ran straight for the snowdrifts. I knew she couldn't keep up. It was 10 degrees below zero. I lost my mittens. When I got home, I had frostbite. We went to the emergency room. "Why didn't you get into the car?" my mother asked. "Always just get into the car."

*

Once when I was in a psychiatric emergency room, I was asked if I thought I had anything to live for, and I said, "My husband and sushi."

The doctor said, joking, "And I hope in that order."

"I really like eel," I said.

*

When I was in high school we lived in a trailer park. My mother lost her job. I took my younger brother to the movies all the time. I insisted we pay in quarters. We had dollar bills. But I wanted to pay with change. For some reason it made me feel rich. I liked giving the cashier the quarters one by one, watching her pause to count my money, ignoring impatient people behind me. This is the most accurate illustration of wealth I can come up with.

*

My first memory: I am nothing larger than a speck. Disembodied hands. Laughing. Coughing. Gagging.

*

When I went to China as part of a foreign exchange program, we visited Confucius's home and the Great Wall. Stuck in America, my boyfriend said he was jealous and then asked, "What is Confucius's home like?"

I said, "It's pretty boring." When we received some pictures from the trip, it was obvious I was not joking. In every photo, I was drifting away from the sight and the other tourists, looking at my watch. He told me that after seeing those pictures, he knew there was no doubt he was in love with me.

*

When I had my first manic episode I was convinced that I had AIDS. I wasn't having sex with anyone. I didn't do drugs. I just knew that something was wrong with me. I went to the emergency room several times. Everyone knew me by name. "I'm dying," I said.

"Why AIDS?" a nurse asked.

"My brain hurts," I said. They believed me. They decided to give me a CT scan. I got on my back as the machine covered my body and closed and locked. Then they told me if I thought I was going to hyperventilate to say something. Knock. "People get scared," they said. "Especially if it's the first time."

It was the first time in months I felt safe. I never wanted to come back out. All I wanted in life was the freedom to knock.

*

I can remember the first time my friend and I went to my favorite high school English teacher's home. She made us lunch. She had so much money. Her backyard contained the hugest hedge maze I had ever seen, even more expansive than the ones in movies. I didn't know the word *hedge maze* at the time. I used the word *labyrinth*. I could tell that made her happy. Who wouldn't want to own their own labyrinth? I wondered if anyone ever got lost in it. "I love puzzles," she said. "Don't you?"

She was an old woman. I imagined that she was very good at figuring things out. I wondered how long she spent in the maze. I wondered if she ever hid from someone in there. My teacher encouraged us to go run up ahead and try to get lost in it. It was easier than I thought. My friend ended up ditching me. I wandered around the paths and looked up at the sky. I pushed against a wall. The hedges were strong and fierce. I shouted for my friend and no one shouted back. It started to feel like the pathways were shrinking. I shut my eyes and imagined that I was in the mind of God.

ACKNOWLEDGMENTS

The author gratefully acknowledges the editors who have selected the following essays to be included in their magazines.

American Literary Review: "On Marxism, My Mother's Body, and the State of Creative Nonfiction"

Another Chicago Magazine: "On Love, Sex, and Thom Gunn"

Clockhouse: "On Beauty"

The Good Men Project: "No"

Mid-American Review: "Ten Anecdotes about the Destruction of Books"

The Normal School: "Self-Portrait as a 1970s Cineplex Movie Theatre (An Abecedarian)"

OCHO: "Deleted Scenes"

Painted Bride Quarterly: "Inspiration"

Pine Hills Review: "My mother is suffering from uterine cancer and all I can think about is the '80s."

Quarterly West: "Are You There Judy? It's Me, Steve."

The Rupture: "I see flies, I see mosquitos, but I have never seen a gay man."

Solstice: "On Apology"

Southern Indiana Review: "On Redemption"

The Sun: "Safe Haven"

Waxwing: "Self-Portrait as a 1980s Cineplex Movie Theatre (An Abecedarian)"

"Self-Portrait as a 1970s Cineplex Movie Theatre" was reprinted in *The Shell Game Anthology* (University of Nebraska Press).

"On Fragmentation" was published in *Bending Genre: Essays on Creative Non-Fiction* (Bloomsbury).

Some additional gratitude I need to express: Thank you to Joy Castro for giving me a place in the Machete series. Thank you to Kristen Elias Rowley for taking a chance on a complete stranger. Also, for editing and reassembling my book. Not to mention dealing with me, which is quite a feat in and of itself. Thank you to Rebecca Bostock for her assistance. Thank you to Mad Creek Books/The Ohio State University Press as a whole. Nicole Walker, your words are an inspiration. In you, I found a mentor I never knew I had. Thank you to Lindsey Brown, who reminds me I'm worth something. Who will write books I'll be jealous of. And Sophia, I still miss being around your words. Zia, what would I do without you? You are an angel, a godsend.

Thank you, Robin, Steven, Michael, and Dinty. Thank you to Melanie Rae Thon for teaching me about the image and life. As you once said, "You write, you rewrite, and then you die." Amen, sister. Thank you to Harlow, Ashley, Carol, Jim, Janie, Cherise, and Dale.

Thank you to SUNY Brockport.

Thanks to S. L. Wisenberg for publishing my first essay and becoming a friend. Special thanks to Bunny Bunny, Bubbles, Bucky, Javelina, Percy, Lullaby Lamb, Christmas Tree, Potato, Honeysuckle Candle, and all the other creatures that bless our home. Thank you, Lydia, for teaching me that true dirty martinis do not exist in western New York.

Thank you to Samantha Ruckman for well, you know, like everything.

Thank you to my mother for teaching me how to survive. Thank you to Eric for teaching me about caregiving. Thank you to Louise Young for being a second mother.

And, of course, Phil, my husband, my polar bear. As you know, the book wouldn't have existed without you. *I* wouldn't exist without you. Thank you for the essay prompts, the editing, the guidance, the fights, the confidence, the endless advice, and the love. It's all about the love. I wouldn't be able to define that word without you. You're my audience, my one.

MACHETE

Joy Castro, Series Editor

This series showcases fresh stories, innovative forms, and books that break new aesthetic ground in nonfiction—memoir, personal and lyric essay, literary journalism, cultural meditations, short shorts, hybrid essays, graphic pieces, and more—from authors whose writing has historically been marginalized, ignored, and passed over. The series is explicitly interested in not only ethnic and racial diversity, but also gender and sexual diversity, neurodiversity, physical diversity, religious diversity, cultural diversity, and diversity in all of its manifestations. The machete enables path-clearing; it hacks new trails and carves out new directions. The Machete series celebrates and shepherds unique new voices into publication, providing a platform for writers whose work intervenes in dangerous ways.